THE
PLOUGH
WOMAN

THE PLOUGH WOMAN

Memoirs of the
Pioneer Women of Palestine

Edited by
RACHEL KATZNELSON SHAZAR
(RUBASHOW)

Translated by
MAURICE SAMUEL

Illustrated

HERZL PRESS   NEW YORK
in conjunction with
PIONEER WOMEN
THE WOMEN'S LABOR ZIONIST ORGANIZATION OF AMERICA

SECOND EDITION

TABLE OF CONTENTS

PART III—AT WORK

PART IV—THE CHILD IN GROUP UPBRINGING

PART V—AMONG WRITERS

ILLUSTRATIONS

APPENDIX

FOREWORD

The Plough Woman originally appeared in English in 1932, and has long been out of print. The present edition once more makes available a fascinating chapter in the history of pioneer Palestine. In addition, in view of the current feminist vogue, it is of special, timely interest.

The title is revealing. "Ploughwoman" is found in neither the Oxford nor Webster dictionaries. "Ploughman" and even "ploughboy" appear under the proper letter, as might be expected, but "ploughwoman" has not made the grade. Conceivably, under the pressure of Women's Lib, which has added non-sexist terms such as the less than felicitous "chairperson" to the language, dictionaries will be revised to include "ploughperson." In any case, it is worth noting that the women workers of Palestine introduced a new concept and a new term into our vocabulary more than fifty years ago. Without any of the fanfare that has accompanied present manifestations of a heightened feminist consciousness, these young women in a desolate corner of the Middle East were a revolutionary vanguard of the movement to liberate women not only politically, but from their own enslavement to conventional attitudes as to the role of women in society.

The young women pioneers who came to Palestine in the early decades of the twentieth century shared the dream of their male comrades: they would create a new egalitarian society in a Jewish homeland, reclaimed through their labor. To this they added still another dimension—the full emancipation of women. In the great task of rebuilding Palestine women were not to be shunted aside into the traditional feminine roles. In her account ("Stages") Rachel Yanait describes the disillusionment that set in when the women discovered that in the tough work of founding a kibbutz in marsh or wasteland, the men undertook the backbreaking jobs of digging roads and clearing rocks, while girls were relegated to the

vii

kitchen and laundry. Such was the indignation of the more ardent feminists among the pioneers that for a brief period kibbutzim consisting solely of women workers sprang up in Galilee, the Emek and on the sands of Judaea. In such kibbutzim there was no danger that women would be denied complete equality in all forms of physical labor. As Rachel puts it, "Nor did they find it so hard to break in the naked soil of the wilderness, if thereby they could slake their thirst for work on the land." The women's kibbutzim were abandoned because they were not practical. A viable agricultural collective required both men and women for psychological as well as economic reasons. This the idealistic young women themselves soon realized, though they did not regret their attempt.

Shortly before the close of World War I, the women suffered another disappointment. When the Jewish Legion was formed, hundreds of young women sought to enlist like the men. Their rejection was a bitter blow: "That rebuff left us flat and wearied; we were not to participate in that great moment." (In this connection we should note that women now serve in the Israeli army, though not in combat.)

In time early feminist extravagances were outgrown. In the course of the subsequent development of Palestine and the kibbutzim, women were to play many and varied roles, as *The Plough Woman* makes clear. Most women themselves stopped demanding the privilege of hewing roads, but neither was the kitchen to be their sole domain. Men took their turn at washing dishes, while women worked in the fields and orchards and developed skills in accordance with their capacities.

Not that the respective roles of women and men were ever sorted out to everybody's satisfaction. The voices heard in *The Plough Woman* keep harping both on the difficulty of fulfilling the desire of women for absolute equality in the choice of work, as well as on the hardships and unforeseen complexities of an existence in which this desire was fulfilled.

As marriages were contracted and children born, the whole nexus of problems related to child-rearing compelled women to reassess their roles. Pregnancy and nursing could not be viewed as discriminatory except at the hand of nature. The establishment of collective children's homes offered an obvious solution to the problem of freeing women from total confinement to private family concerns. Yet while the children's home enabled women to play their part in the total life of the kibbutz, women, not men, were entrusted with the care of young children. This division of labor coincided with the desires of most women and sprang from their intimate experience as mothers.

Some of the problems examined by the writers sound as modern as the latest issue of *Ms* Magazine. Women drawn to political activities and with no recourse to the shelter of the kibbutz were tormented by a familiar theme: Were they sacrificing their families to their careers? In the brief chapter, "Borrowed Mothers," the writer describes her maternal anguish at leaving her children for tasks she views as important. With devastating honesty she admits that a "borrowed mother," even if kind and efficient, is not a wholly satisfactory substitute and that her children suffer. She writes: "The modern woman asks herself: Is there something wrong with me if my children don't fill up my life? . . . Can we today measure devotion to husband and children by our indifference to everything else?" The signatory is G.M., Golda Myerson, later to be known as Golda Meir.

The Plough Woman is a vivid, personal record of remarkable women in a heroic time. The present edition has not been revised or updated. It speaks for itself. The only change from the original text has been the omission of a section, "The Departed," consisting of memorials to young comrades who died or were killed in the arduous period which the book so movingly records. To make *The Plough Woman* more useful to the contemporary reader, biographical notes and a glossary, prepared by Gertrude Hirschler, assistant editor of the Herzl Press,have been added, as well as an epilogue by Beba Idelson, long the head of *Moetzet Hapoalot,* the Council of Women Workers of Israel.

MARIE SYRKIN

1975

INTRODUCTION

THIS book is, in form and content, the mirror of a great episode in the history of Jewish womanhood. It is not a literary enterprise. It is a simple collection of human documents, a co-operative effort to record, in direct personal reports, the spirit and achievements of a generation of women.

For the last few years the Jewish women workers of Palestine have felt a deep inner need to set down in writing the story of their movement; and in 1928 the Council of the Women Workers of Palestine decided to issue the collective volume which here appears in English under the name of *The Plough Woman*. Four leading motives were responsible for this resolution. First, the desire to make an accounting of the achievements of the women workers of Palestine and to arrive at an accurate evaluation of their worth; second, to put into permanent form certain important incidents in the history of the new Palestine; third, to acquaint the Jewish youth throughout the world with that part of our labor history which is represented by the second and third immigration streams into Palestine (1904 to 1924); fourth, to achieve a greater degree of self-understanding by means of self-expression.

It would have been impossible to achieve these ends merely through a series of abstract articles by specialists. We needed the personal records of those who had been a living part of the process. And therefore some fifty women comrades, nearly all of them engaged in agricultural work in the communes, individualist settlements and training farms of Palestine, were invited to participate in what

xi

might be called the upbuilding of the book. The eagerness
with which the Jewish public in Palestine and outside has
accepted the Hebrew and Yiddish editions has convinced
us that the method which was employed in putting together these records was the right one.

The original work was naturally in Hebrew, and was
issued by the Council of the Women Workers in Palestine; the first translation, in Yiddish, was published in
America under the auspices of the Pioneer Women's Organization, a branch of the Poale Zion, the Socialist-
Zionist Party. This body is also responsible for the publication of the work in English. In this way an original
source is opened to the English reading public which
may acquaint itself at first hand with the life of the Jewish
women workers of Palestine, one of the most important
and fascinating chapters in the new history of that
country.

In the structure of the book an attempt is made to cover
systematically the principal problems and aspects of the
women workers' movement.

The first section, *In the Beginning*, covers the period of
the Second Immigration—1904-1914. It deals with the
struggle of the Jewish woman who was adapting herself
to an unwonted form of physical labor, with her ac-
climatisation to a new world, a new nature and new life-
forms.

The section *With the Group* deals with the relationship of the individual woman to the labor movement in
general, and to the specific group to which she happened
to be attached in particular; it is a singular story of the
self-sacrifice of the one for the many, of the integration
of personal lives with the larger life of the community.

At Work describes the struggle of the woman worker
to find an acknowledged place in the ranks of labor, the
rise of her specific forms of settlement in town and village, and her economic and social achievements. To some
extent this section crosses with the one that follows—
The Child in Group Upbringing—for the problems of the

xii

family, of the upbringing of children stand in close and inevitable relationship to those of work and social achievement.

The last section, *Among Writers,* does not purport to give anything like a picture of the cultural productivity of the Jewish women workers of Palestine. It is a reminder, rather than a record; for it was impossible to make the book complete without such a reminder and equally impossible to do anything more within these limits. In the same way, the section *The Departed* is the briefest indication, chosen out of a long list of heroic figures, of the sacrifices which have been laid on the altar of Jewish freedom. The women whose lives were broken in the struggle are legion; the few remembered here are representative and not exceptional.

RACHEL KATZNELSON-RUBASHOW (SHAZAR)

1932

xiii

TRANSLATOR'S NOTE

THE translation of this book was at once easy and difficult. It was easy because this is a forthright and simple record, without affectations and attempts to be impressive; it was exceptionally difficult because of the recurrence of terms which can be translated literally but cannot be made to convey their true meaning.

The new Jewish homeland has already produced a life with traditional forms; and formal names for certain institutions have already become charged with a unique and intransferable quality. The word *Shomer* can only be translated as "guard," or "watchman"; and yet the bald translation is quite as meaningless for the English reader, quite as void of the significance of the term as, let us say, a literal translation of the word *cowboy* into French or German. For the American cowboy of the past is not just a function; he is a tradition, a part of history, a heritage and a peculiarity. He is a unique type and institution. And the *Shomer* of Palestine represents now in Jewish life a similar untranslatable phenomenon, a unique product of time and place and will, concentrating within himself a whole world of memories and experiences. He was a symbol of Jewish self-defence, of Jewish emergence from dependence, of Jewish pride. The thrill of the word must be understood not against the background of romantic adventurousness, but against a more significant background of a national renaissance and a repudiation of an unhappy past.

For the word *kvutzah* I have occasionally used the literally exact but spiritually inadequate translation *commune*. But the *kvutzah* and the *kibutz*, two Palestinian forms of commune, have a special power in their own setting, and to reach that power the whole setting must be understood. They are, in social form, communes, but their relation to the Jewish national movement, to the cultural revival, to the Palestinian life, turned them into rich, new human experiments; they have acquired, for the Palestinian Jew, inner, subtle values which simple translation cannot convey.

And for this reason I have found myself compelled to leave the words in the original, adding explanations from time to time, and trusting that the total effect of this book will ultimately convey the full power of these words. A time may come when these words will acquire a certain international currency, when the world will be sufficiently acquainted with the Jewish homeland in Palestine to have direct access to its values; when the *Chalutz* will be something more than a pioneer, the *Shomer* more than a guard, the *kvutzah* more than a commune, the *meshek hapoaloth* more than a women's training farm. Every civilisation produced high types and institutions which, in their ideal form, are added to the world's collection of models: among these are to be found, to this day, the products of the Palestinian Jewish life of two thousand years ago; among these, in the future, will also be found the products of the Palestinian Jewish life of today. It is therefore perhaps as well to anticipate that time by accepting their word-symbols now.

The casual reader will occasionally be puzzled by differences the existence of which he did not suspect—the difference, for instance, between a 'colonist" and a worker. Here again the historic background is needed as explanation. The Jewish labor movement of Palestine began only in the twentieth century; Jewish colonisation before that time was almost exclusively of the "planter" type. The struggle of the Jewish land-worker to find a place for himself in the agricultural economy ran up against the opposition of the old individualist planters who had built their system on the use of cheap, exploited and unorganised

Arab labor. In the twentieth century the two types of
Jewish colonisation went on side by side, with the worker
type (representing also a specific social idealism cast in
specific forms) on the increase. The struggle between the
two types is recorded, among other things, in these pages;
and the gradual infiltration of Jewish labor into Jewish
colonies is an important chapter in the integration of the
Jewish homeland.

At one extreme was the *moshavah*, the settlement of
purely individualist farms and planters; at the other extreme the *kvutzah*, or commune; in between was the *moshav
ovdim*, the individualist settlement in which each family
worked its own plot, did not exploit the labor of others,
and developed a high degree of cooperation with the other
families in the settlement. Behind these colonies must
be understood also the background of the national institutions, the Zionist Organization, the Jewish Labor Federation of Palestine, and the various instruments of these
organisations. It would confuse rather than help the
reader to load his attention at the outset with lists and
glossaries. It happens that the pages which follow are
so fascinating in a purely human way that the reader's
attention will be held even where he cannot always pick
his way through the allusions. As he reads on, however, the picture will clarify itself in his mind; he will
gradually and without effort acquire a general picture
of the country behind the individual figures which will
claim his first attention. More than that, he will begin to
appreciate, perhaps for the first time, the extraordinary
folk-depths of the movement, the deep and inexhaustible
sources of a renaissance which, in effect, is only at its
beginning.

MAURICE SAMUEL

1932

PART I
IN THE BEGINNING

I

IN THE BEGINNING
THE COLLECTIVE

In the spring of 1904 I became acquainted with Ezekiel Chankin's *kvutzah*, or commune, in the colony of Rechoboth. I had by that time determined to find out what it was that the country meant to *me*, as an individual. My plan was to make a tour of the Jewish colonies and to get together such statistics as were available. The task took up a year of my time. I worked out a questionnaire which covered the economic side of colony life. I asked in particular for details of income, and the employment of Arab workers. Few indeed were the colonists who at that time kept statistics of their own. But I became acquainted with the character of our first *Aliah*, or immigration; and I came to a definite conclusion. My comrades—the workers—were completely mad! *The way they were working there was absolutely no hope of creating in Palestine a Jewish agricultural proletariat!*

The Jewish workers in the colony of Petach Tikvah had accepted the same conditions as the Arabs: their pay was 5 piastres (25 cents) a day. They believed that as Zionists they simply had not the right to ask for more. They lived eight in a room—a small room—and their beds were mattresses on the floor. When I told them that they ought to demand houses and public buildings from the colony they answered proudly that this would be philanthropy . . . They would ask for no help from these sources: it would only be a renewal of the immemorial evil of the *Chalukkah* —the charity system for Palestinian Jewry.

Finally the Jewish workers of Petach Tikvah were driven by sheer need to live in a commune, or collective. There was no other way out for them. Their collective was the second in Palestine, and the first was Chankin's collective in Rechoboth.

I had already had some experience with a collective—in Minsk. A group of us wanted to organise the workers without the help of the intelligentsia, and to that end we started a collective. The life was harsh and meagre, and the budget was between three and five kopecks (a kopeck was half a cent) per day per person. All earnings were turned in to the common fund. It was while living with this collective that I learned an important principle: the collective provides the proletariat with the means for its struggle. The Minsk commune prepared me for the collectives of Palestine.

I began on my arrival in Palestine with an urban co-operative, for I was more accustomed to city conditions. In Russia I had learned carpentry in the factory of my brother, Gedaliah Wilbushevitch. I raised a loan in order to start a carpenters' cooperative in Jaffa, and I worked out its rules on the basis of the Russian *artels*, which had a communist background. The cooperative existed for three months. When I left for Galilee internal dissensions broke out and the cooperative fell to pieces.

In the year 1905 Joshua Chankin spoke to me about the possibility of buying up the Emek, or Valley of Jezreel, and it was clear to me that only through such a purchase could a Jewish agricultural class be established in Palestine. I was anxious to help Chankin, and I placed before him my plans for collectivist colonisation. Meanwhile Jewish immigration into Palestine kept growing.

I then made up my mind to go to Paris and approach the Jewish Colonisation Association—the I. C. A., founded by Baron Hirsh—to buy land in the Emek for workers' colonisation. I also wanted to do some research in Paris on various attempts which have been made at collectivist colonisation. There I came across a cousin of mine, Ivan Wilbushevitch, who was editing the government organ for the French colonies. Through him I obtained access to

the material of the government departments on the colonisation in Tunis and Algeria.

I realised soon enough that what I had in mind was not
to be found anywhere. Indeed, the experts considered
agricultural collectivism ridiculous, and were ready to
prove that the agricultural commune had never been able
to succeed.

At about that time a Jewish comrade of mine, arriving
from Russia, asked me to help him raise money for the
Jewish self-defence in that country. I collected two hundred thousand francs for that purpose—fifty thousand of
it coming from Baron Edmond de Rothschild—and helped
him, further, to smuggle arms into Russia.

I re-entered Russia illegally. During the pogrom in
Shedlitz I took an active part in the Jewish self-defence.
Later I organised a national group to exact vengeance from
the leaders of Russian anti-Semitism. One of the comrades
in the group was Pinchas Dashevsky, who shot the famous
anti-Semite Krushevan. The entire group was arrested—
with the exception of Dashevsky. Again the traitor was
Azeff, who got his information through two Socialist Rev-
olutionaries who worked with us. The police looked for
me in St. Petersburg. I changed my lodgings every day
never sleeping twice in the same place. With clockwork
regularity the police always searched, too late, the place
I had slept in the night before. My name was unknown to
them.

I worked for three months with "The Group of Vengeance." The only Jewish party which supported us was
the Territorialist, the party which was looking for a Jewish homeland elsewhere than in Palestine. Later, toward
the end of 1906, I returned to Palestine via Constantinople.

Once again I turned to my comrades with the old idea
of a collective. I wanted to go to America to raise money
for collective colonisation in Transjordania and in the
Hauran, north of Palestine. I also planned to visit the
American collectivist colonies.

Early in 1907 I arrived in America and spent nearly half
a year there. I became acquainted with Dr. Judah L.
Magnes and with Henrietta Szold. I visited South America, too, taking in the collectivist colonies, and convinced
myself at first hand that the agricultural commune could
succeed. What we needed was a substitute for the religious enthusiasm which had made these settlements possible, and for this substitute I looked to Socialism.

In August, 1907, I returned to Palestine via Paris. I had
one ideal now—the realisation of agricultural collectivism.
During my absence the idea had taken somewhat deeper
root in Palestine. In the colonies of Lower Galilee the
Jewish workers lived wretched, disorganised lives. They
were housed in stables. Some of them had already lost all
faith in the burning ideal of "the Conquest of Labor"—the
upbuilding of the country by the working class. They
could not become individualist farmers, planters, exploiters
of others; their Socialist principles forbade it. And they
could not continue their competition with Arab labor, for
no European can long subsist on five piastres a day. I, for
my part, had never believed in the Conquest of Labor
through adaptation to the Arab standard of life.

At that time the National Fund had begun to purchase
land as the inalienable property of the Jewish people. The
ideal of national territory of this kind had always been
close to my heart, for I saw in it the foundation of collectivist colonisation. Eliezer Shochat was against my plan.
His argument was: "We daren't assume this responsibility. If the particular plan which we adopt for collectivist
colonisation fails, we shall lose faith in the ideal of colonisation as such. The first thing we must learn is to become
land workers."

In the farm of the ICA (Jewish Colonisation Association) at Sedjera there were comrades of ours working under the direction of the agronomist Krause. Every year this
farm showed a deficit. I said to the ICA: "Give us a

chance to work here on our own responsibility, and we'll manage without a deficit."

The opportunity was given us. At Sedjera, I worked half-days on the books and the other half-days in the cow-barn. I told Krause that he ought to admit women to the work, and the first three women workers there were the sisters Shturman, Sarah (Krigser), Shifra (Betzer) and Esther (Becker). They were all very young, and they followed the plough like real peasants.

When we founded the collective we were eighteen in all who had drifted together gradually toward Sedjera. The contract with the agronomist Krause turned over to us the field and dairy work on the same terms as were demanded of an Arab lessee. The owners gave us all the dead and live stock, the inventory and the seed. In return we had to turn over one-fifth of the harvest. We were also given sleeping quarters—and very poor ones they were—and a sum of money to carry us through the season. When there was not enough work on the farm to go round, the management would employ some of us in the afforestation work.

We worked on our own responsibility. We arranged our own division of labor. Only once a week, when the program was planned, we would have Krause in for a consultation. We also asked him to give regular lectures on agriculture, and no one who lived with us through that time has forgotten those clear and practical expositions.

The workers on the farm did not have a kitchen of their own, and until the coming of the collective they used to eat out. We organised a communal kitchen, and later on we were even able to feed workers not belonging to our commune.

The name we gave ourselves was, simply, "The Collective." The relations between us and the other workers on the farm were excellent. But they had no faith in our plan and did not believe we would come out without a deficit.

The Sedjera Collective lasted a year and a half. It ended its work successfully, paid the farm its fifth of the harvest, returned in full the money that had been advanced, and demonstrated once for all that a collective economy was a possibility.

K'far Gileadi   MANYA SHOCHAT.

THOSE FIRST YEARS

WHEN I came to Petach Tikvah in 1905 some Jewish workers were already there. There were only four girls among them: two seamstresses, one stocking knitter, and one who received remittances from her parents. In the season both seamstresses would turn orange packers. But my heart was set on plain labor on the soil. Three days after my arrival I went out to work with the spade for one bishlik (twelve and a half cents) a day. I worked in Gissin's vineyard, and my job was to fill up the holes around the trees.

I used to come home evenings to the colony without any tools, and for a whole month I would leave the regular path and make my way through backyards, so that no one should know that I was working with the men. The workers themselves were against my choice—they were genuinely afraid that I would break down under the labor. They urged me to work with the other girls at the orange packing—but I would not listen. I wanted to work with the spade.

It was comrade S. who first gave me courage to continue. He was the teacher in the colony; and he shifted the school hours so as to be able to come out and take turns with me at the work. In this way, while our comrades took only one hour's rest during the middle of the day, I took three. S. also talked about me to the owner of the vineyard, who assured him that in time I would become a good worker.

Two weeks later the owner raised my pay by half a piastre—making a full three piastres a day. I was astonished, and asked him whether he had done this because I was a Jewish girl or because I was really worth it. He answered frankly that I was really worth a great deal more.

And yet for a long time I was tormented by the question whether I had chosen the right path. The doubts of my fellow-workers crept into me too, and I needed someone who would give me more faith in myself and in my own strength.

There worked among us at that time a comrade who was much older than any of us—the man who later became famous in Palestine as A. D. Gordon. His good humor and unflagging cheerfulness were a source of strength to all of us. He composed a great many Jewish songs, which we learned to sing together with him. From the beginning I conceived a deep affection for this old man—but I had not the courage to seek his advice. Often, seeing me sit apart, completely exhausted, he would call out to me: "Cheer up! Look at me, an old man, working as hard as the rest, and always happy." But before I could answer him, and pour out my troubles, he would be gone.

My work with the spade lasted a month, and after that I passed over to orange picking. During the first two days I worked for nothing. When my first basket was filled, I submitted it to the overseer, who went through it, orange by orange. He found three which had been touched by the scissors. My heart was in my mouth—I was certain he would send me home. But in the second basket there was only one damaged orange—and from then on I was a perfect orange picker. When my work on this orchard was finished the overseer sent me to a second. I became known as a skilled orange picker, and work was easy to find.

When the season was over I went to the employment bureau of the colony to look for work. I was told that there were only three colonists who were prepared to take women workers, and none of them had a place for me.

For the second time I was seized with despair. I came home, and sat down in loneliness, and brooded over the

life I had chosen for myself. I remembered then the letters
which I had received from a well known Zionist leader
before I set out for Palestine. He had warned me against
coming to Palestine. "You will find no work there," he
wrote, "you will suffer hunger and want, and no one will
be any the better for it."

For three days I sought work in vain, and at the end
of the third day, when I sat again in my room, beaten,
the old man came to me. He invited me over to his little
shack, and there we talked for many, many hours. He
gave me courage to hold out; and in the next few days I
found employment, together with him. He became my
teacher in the work.

Before long I was dissatisfied with the simple work; I
wanted the more responsible task of grafting trees. A comrade undertook to teach me. He told me to lay off work
with the spade for a couple of days, and to bring him his
meals in the orchard. At that hour the owner was away,
and he would then be able to show me how to graft. I fell
in with this plan. Two days later the worker told his boss
that I was a skilful grafter, and that I had already been
employed for that purpose in other orchards. The owner
took me on trial, was satisfied with me, and let me remain.

When I had been working for a year and a half I was
told that another woman land-worker had appeared in
Rechoboth—Miriam Zavin. And in 1907 several other
women workers came from Russia and went up to Galilee,
to work on the farm of Sedjera.

I worked in Petach Tikvah for a total of three years,
till 1908. Some time before the end of that year a group
of our men workers had gone up to the farm of Kinereth.
They applied to the director to let me join them—but not
in the kitchen, as was the almost invariable rule with
women. Up in Kinereth I worked side by side with the
men. First I helped to clear the soil of stones, later I
took a hand in the mowing and threshing. There were no

houses for.the workers in those days. In the summer we
slept out in the open. In the winter the woman who worked
in the kitchen and I slept in the barn. Raids and attacks
by our neighbors were fairly frequent in those days

With the beginning of the new year the two of us
joined the little *kvutzah* or commune which began to work
on its own initiative and responsibility in Um-Djuni. And
there at last I began to feel that I had become a full-
fledged worker. The year's work in Um-Djuni ended
with a profit, and yet for a variety of reasons the group
fell to pieces. A second group came up to the same ground.
I was away then, being down for several months with
yellow fever. When I recovered I joined the new group—
and out of this group grew the present settlement of
Deganiah.

Nahalal   TECHIAH LIBERSON.

IN SEDJERA

THE farm of Sedjera has long since been abandoned But there was a time when it occupied a highly important place in the life of the Jewish workers of Palestine. When the first Jewish women workers came to Galilee, it was Sedjera that took them in. It was in Sedjera that the first Jewish guards appeared, and it was there that *Ha-Shomer*, the organisation of Jewish guards, was founded. In Sedjera, too, the first attempt was made to organise the Jewish working class of Palestine. *Ha-Choresh* (the Plowman) was the name given to that first tiny organisation of land workers.

Sedjera played a great role in our life; and in the few years of its existence as the focal point of the workers of Galilee exacted a heavy toll of sacrifices.

I came to Sedjera in 1907, and found there only four Jewish workers from Europe. The others were Kurdistan Jews.

When I left the town for the farm, I had not the slightest idea what I was going to do there. No city girl was ever remoter from land work than I. And in those days there was of course no *Chalutz* (Pioneer) organisation to prepare the newcomer for life in Palestine.

Krause, the manager of the Sedjera farm (he has for many years since then been director of the agricultural school of Mikveh Israel) was very friendly toward Jewish labor in general and toward the Jewish woman worker in particular. Every opportunity was given on the farm to the worker who wanted to learn a special branch of agriculture.

On the first day I was set to sifting barley after the old Arab fashion. My companion in the work was a Kurdistan

Jew. But I found this task too monotonous. I wanted something livelier and more significant. In particular I wanted to go in for dairy work, but I knew absolutely nothing about it. I did not even know how to begin learning something. Without experience, without a plan, I simply went ahead.

The first thing I did was to clean out and whitewash the little room in the barn. The dairy vessels were of the most primitive kind. All day long the farm flock, consisting of sheep and goats, pastured in the neighboring woods. A deaf and dumb Arab was the shepherd. Twice a day he brought me the milk to turn into cheese. Bringing it he would point to his black mantel if it came from the goats, and to his white *kefia* if it came from the sheep.

I took my first lesons in cheesemaking from the womenfolk of the old colonists. And in time I became as it were the official dairy worker.

After a while I was joined in Sedjera by my two younger sisters and their two friends. One of the girls took over the kitchen work: the other three insisted on going out with the plough. They did not keep up this labor for long; but those first days belonged to a young and happy time.

Later on Manya Schochat came to Sedjera, and the first working class collective in Palestine was founded. And so, step by step, the Sedjera farm expanded into something like a settlement.

Nahalal   SHIFRA BETZER.

THE JEWISH GUARD

THIS was twenty years ago in the colony of K'far Tabor
(Meschah) in Galilee. After long negotiations with the
council the *Ha-Shomer* organisation took over the guard-
ing of the colony on condition that Jewish labor be introduced.

Up till then the Jewish colonists had employed Arab
labor exclusively, and the Arabs, living with their families
in the yards of the colonies, knew every corner in the place;
it was, therefore, impossible to put a stop to the thefts.
The workers inside the colony frequently cooperated with
the outside thieves. The colonists knew this well, yet it
was no light task to persuade them to take Jewish labor.
Finally a contract was signed, and Jewish workers entered
the colony together with the Jewish guards.

According to the agreement the guards and workers
came up into the colony in the month of Elul (September).
The *Shomrim* or guards were given, as headquarters, the
last house in the village, standing on the last parcel of
Jewish soil. The workers were distributed among the
colonists and thus provided with lodgings and food. In
the course of one year they were supposed to become skilled
laborers.

The first evening of the watch. The patrols are out.
Every man has instructions, he knows the extent of his
beat, he has learned by heart the whistle signals which
carry the alarm from place to place. One of the women
workers, S., told a friend that she did not want to work
in the kitchen: she loved the silence and the darkness of
the night, she loved weapons and horses, and she wanted
to join the guard. The young man had confidence in her.
He obtained weapons for her, also an Arab *abaya* (cloak)

and a whistle. When nightfall came they told no one, but rode out to their posts, and divided the beat between them. In those days the Jewish colonies in Galilee were ringed in by walls. The young man took the eastern side of the colony; the woman took the western side.

When the first rounds had been finished it was the custom for the guards to meet and report, and the presence of the woman was discovered. The comrades were somehow pleased by the idea: all except one, who argued that this sort of thing could not go on. "We must not forget," he said, "that we may have clashes with the Arabs—and particularly with the men who were employed as guards before we came." The man's objections were received in silence—and the woman remained at her post. But it was decided to let no one in the colony know.

With the coming of the Jewish guards and the Jewish workers a new spirit was born in the colony. There was singing and dancing in the evenings. The children of the settler colonists—a handful of youngsters—were drawn toward the Jewish workers. The apathy which had brooded over the place was dispersed, and those colonists who had fought for the Jewish guards felt themselves completely vindicated.

The guards were at their posts from early evening until six in the morning. All night long they circled the walls on the *qui vive,* listening for the slightest stirring out in the fields. A whisper, a faint motion, a glimmer somewhere, and the nerves jumped. On the first round they tried all the gates and doors. On later rounds they focussed their attention on the surrounding fields.

One night, during the second round, the *shomer* noticed that a stall had been opened. He loaded his gun and entered the yard. Suddenly he perceived in the darkness two Arabs driving animals before them. He shot three times and the Arabs fled. Cases of this kind were frequent before winter came; and on one occasion the thieves were able to get away with a couple of mules. Then the *Shomer* organisation insisted that Arabs who did not live in the village, but who came there only for the day's work, should not be allowed to stay overnight. So, step by step, the epidemic of thieving was combatted.

The first year of the Jewish guard in Meschah passed peacefully, and the contract was renewed. *Ha-Shomer* extended its work to the neighboring Jewish colony of Jabniel, and S.'s friend went out on the new patrol.

One night soon after, S. was kept awake until early morning by a strange feeling of oppression. And before daybreak news was brought from Jabniel that there had been a clash. One Arab had been killed, and S.'s friend had been severely wounded. S. saddled her mare, put on her *abaya,* slung her gun over her shoulder and set out for Jabniel. She forgot, in her anxiety, that Jabniel lay five or six hours away, that in between the two colonies there was not a single Jewish post, and that the road was dangerous. She rode at top speed, obsessed only by one thought: Would she find her friend still alive? Many Arabs pass her on the way. They do not stop her. She only hears them asking each other, as she rides by: "Isn't that a woman?"

One hour still remains between her and Jabniel, and she sees the colony in the distance. And now a well dressed Arab on a richly caparisoned horse comes riding toward her. He stops her and asks:

"Where are you going? Shall I accompany you?"

"No."

The Arab becomes angry.

"Do you want to quarrel with me?" he asks.

He comes closer, spurring his horse forward till it touches hers. Suddenly S. reaches for the man's cloak and pulls him out of his saddle. He tumbles to earth, and she shoots forward. By the time he has remounted she is too far ahead to be followed. They are close to the boundary of the Jewish colony.

In Jabniel there was talk of an Arab attack, and the

Jews had sent out for help to the neighboring colonies. Many members of *Ha-Shomer* responded, but none attracted the same attention as S., in her Arab mantle, her gun over her shoulder, her ammunition belt round her. The colonists' daughters in partciular were astounded by this woman in arms. That night S. took an active part in the defence of the colony.

The colony of Jabniel was in fact too small to carry a public expense. In the end the ICA (Jewish Colonisation Association) decided to increase its area. Neighboring land was purchased. The deeds were signed and delivered, but it was impossible to start ploughing the purchased land without armed forces. The government forbade the Jews the use of arms, but was in no particular hurry to extend its own protection. Every new acquisition of land brought its own sacrifices.

For a long time after the first Jabniel purchases the rains fell, and ploughing was out of the question. When the rain stopped twenty workers with ten pairs of mules and with wagons full of ploughs and other implements were sent up to Jabniel. Early one morning they set out toward the fields in long Indian file, ready to draw the first furrow. Along with the workers went the Jewish guards. And so while some followed the plough, others on horseback kept circling round the new soil.

Broad daylight came, and the ploughers were already far afield, when we saw the entire Arab village coming toward us, men and women, young and old.

We, the women, stood in the yard of the Jewish colony, and watched the whole scene from a distance. The Arab crowd drew nearer and nearer to the workers. At last one of the *shomrim* stopped them. An Arab stepped out from the crowd to argue with him, and after a long talk turned back to consult the others.

We watched the crowd advance once more, and once more the riders blocked their path. The workers in the fields, behind the riders, ignored the proceedings. They carried on as if nothing were happening, and the furrows grew longer and longer behind them. At last the Arab crowd turned back. All day long, without stopping to rest or eat, the Jewish workers ploughed the new fields.

In the evening they returned. But scarcely had they given fodder to the horses when a runner came from another part of the colony. Arabs had attacked the colonists as these were returning from the fields. Hot on the heels of the runner came a second. The colony was being encircled.

Without waiting, the men set out for the scene of the attack. A strange thing had happened. The Arabs had captured the Jewish workers, undressed them—and left them naked. . .

For two weeks the colony lived in a state of siege. Finally the government sent help, and also gave us permission to use our arms. From that time on life became quieter and more secure.

Ain Charod   Chaya-Sarah Chankin.

THE FOUNDING OF MERCHAVIAH

A LITTLE while ago I made a journey from Nablus to Nahalal. Many years had passed since I had been this way. From Nablus to Jenin everything looked much as it had looked: the chief difference was the smooth road which had replaced the narrow, stony paths, so that Afule could be reached in four hours instead of in twenty-four. But beyond Jenin the Emek, the Valley of Jezreel, was absolutely unrecognisable. A host of memories awoke in me as I looked on the Jewish settlements—many of them unknown to me even by name—which were now scattered through the great valley. And closing my eyes, I could conjure up the Emek as it once had been, with its solitary Jewish settlement of Merchaviah in the centre.

It was in 1909 that Joshuah Chankin purchased from some rich Effendis the territory of Fuleh. Fellaheen, Arab peasants, used to work that soil before "at a fifth"; that is to say, the Effendi would provide them with seed and with implements, and in payment would take four-fifths of the harvest. The peasant retained the remaining fifth.

To the new settlement which we started in Fuleh, the Jews gave the name of Merchaviah, from the Hebrew for "broadness of God"; for the broad acres of the valley stretched far and wide on every side of the settlement.

Even before the signing of the deeds Chankin proposed to the *Choresh* (Plowman), the Workers' Organisation of Galilee, to put together a *kvutzah*, or commune, to go up to the new ground. The organisation began at once, and happy were the few men and women who were permitted to join. The territory of Merchaviah was small, and not more than thirty workers were needed for it. It took many meetings and endless debates before the personnel was

chosen. A great privilege lay before it: the preparation of
a new Jewish position, the laying of the foundations of a
permanent settlement. Twenty-six men went out and four
women.

The comrades of *Ha-Shomer* had already discharged
this task of preliminary occupation and work in many of
the colonies of Galilee. The men and women for Merchaviah were therefore chosen mostly from its ranks. The
meeting place for the comrades was in Kinereth, then the
centre for the settlements of Galilee. And there they
waited for their supplies and for the order.

But things went slowly. The Arab peasants, who had
accepted a heavy money indemnity, refused to leave the
soil. Meanwhile five comrades went up to Damascus to
purchase implements and returned after a week with carts-
ful of ploughs, saddles, harness, straw mats, threshing-
sleds and the rest. Those of us who waited in Kinereth
were quartered on the farm. We were received with open
arms, even though life had been hard enough before our
coming. Meals had to be served in three sittings. We slept
on straw, either in garrets or in the open yard. But everything seemed good to us; Merchaviah was waiting.

Week after week went by, and still we remained in Kinereth, waiting for marching orders which never came.
Some of our comrades worked on the Kinereth farm, and
others were occupied with the work of our group. Our
presence became a genuine burden to our hosts. There
was not only ourselves; there were the mules, which crowded those of the Kinereth farmers. Human beings, we
argued, can put up with a great deal—but mules must be
taken care of. . . I myself was not in Kinereth with the
first, but I became sick of waiting among my chickens in
Jabniel. I too went up to Kinereth. But it was clear by
now that we were abusing the friendliness of the Kinereth
farmers. We made up our minds to relieve our hosts. We
"set up house" for ourselves in the open on the shore of the
Sea of Galilee. But the mules had to be left in the stable,

for fear of thieves. We did our cooking between two stones under a tree. There we ate, and there we did our washing, waiting with infinite patience for the word of release.   And after three months of vagabondage, of gypsy life in the open, we got our orders.

A day of that kind stays in the memory forever. A week before our release Chankin sent up three men, who spoke Arabic well, to Merchaviah. It was their task to reach an understanding with the Arabs, so that we might occupy our territory in peace. We wanted to avoid quarrels with our neighbors, and we wanted to avoid government intervention. When the week had passed word came to us to prepare for the journey. By ten in the morning we were ready with all our worldly goods.

There was joy in Kinereth and in all the Jewish colonies around. The workers of Kinereth went with us part of the way, and with them many of the colonists from surrounding settlements; and so a great crowd, on foot and on horseback, accompanied the slowly moving wagons when they set out. The procession went singing all the way up the slope to Puriah; and there we parted, with many benedictions, with songs and with firing of shots, as the custom was in those days.

In the evening we came to Merchaviah, and found the three comrades who had preceded us. And now the grimmer task began. Our first accommodation was in the abandoned, half-ruined Arab huts of clay, which were infested with vermin. But more important than ourselves were the mules. Better quarters had to be found for them. And the sowing had to begin without delay, for with the long waiting at Kinereth we had advanced far into the season.

We chose for our "public" buildings an Arab yard containing three huts, of which the largest was twelve by eighteen in size. This one we turned into kitchen and dining hall. There was no furniture. One-half of the floor was nearly two feet higher than the other. So we called the higher half "the table," and the kitchen was set up on the lower half. Round the walls there were clay troughs in which the Arabs used to cover up the fodder for the cattle. These we converted into our stores. Having no stove we cooked on stones outside. In the two small huts we kept our supplies and our fowl.

There was work in abundance for the women, and no orders were necessary. But two of them were incapacitated, because they were expecting children, and a double burden therefore fell on myself and the fourth. And yet, in spite of the heaviness of our tasks, we could not live entirely without some attempt at "adornment." What irked us most was our "table," even when we covered it with straw matting. True, there was plenty of fun about eating at this table, for there were very few among our comrades who could squat like Arabs, with legs crossed underneath. The others, in spite of their efforts, could never get the hang of it. So either they knelt at table or ate lying on the floor. We whitewashed the inside of the huts, and brought in flowers. And finally we rose to the dignity of a table: we found a few boards, laid them on a trestle, and achieved equality with all other Jewish settlements in Palestine. Around this banqueting board we set empty gasolene cans, and more boards on top of these. We bought white oilcloth in Haifa, and finally our dining hall took on that appearance which was for so many years characteristic of all the *kvutzoth*.

Then came the question of bread. The *kvutzah* was still without its own oven. Fresh bread was brought daily from Haifa, the reason being that there was no bakery big enough to prepare several days' supply. The bread was of poor quality—more like dough than bread; and we saw that we would have to do our own baking. The difficulties were simply incredible. The Arab "oven"—called a *tuban* —was a primitive contrivance which was kept smoking all night long; in the morning the thin Arab cakes were laid on the glowing ashes. Most of the *tubans* in the village were broken. We found one that could still be used, and on this we used to bake.

It was a marvelous sort of business. We could not wait until the *tuban* had stopped smoking, because the bread was needed first thing in the morning, and as soon as the first lot was ready, the second had to be started. So we had to lay out the loaves while the *tuban* was still filled with hot ashes and smoke. After every separate loaf we had to run out to catch breath. Squatting inside that oven we were nearly suffocated. Getting out in time was not easy either, for the interior was black with swirling smoke, and more than once, making a blind rush for the entrance, we cracked our heads against the walls. It was two months before the men could get enough leisure to put up an oven with a chimney.

During those first months of the sowing our "dining hall" was jammed. Our own group could not plough and plant the whole stretch, and men had to be brought in from the colonies. There were often as many as fifty mouths to fed—not counting the tourists who used to drop in on us. Between meals we had to find time for the washing of our comrades' clothes. Finally two women joined us: a worker and a *feldsherin*, a first-aid pharmacist and doctor; and then the work became easier.

That new district, the great, open space of the Emek, the Valley of Jezreel, awoke a deep and permanent love in me. More than once I longed to leave the kitchen and join the line of the comrades who were driving the first Jewish plough through the Emek; for it seemed to me that there was no greater happiness than this in all the world.

Meshek Ha-Poaloth,
  Shechunath Boruchov   ESTHER BECKER.

WITH THE SHOMRIM IN GALILEE

THERE was a rule in *Ha-Shomer*—the organisation of Jewish guards —that every comrade had to remain foot-loose, ready for duty in any place. It was not unusual for a *Shomer* to change his post a dozen times in one year, and wind up where he began. A man had hardly settled in one place before he was sent on to another. On the surface it was an easy life: six gasolene cans and four planks made up the family furniture. Food and lodging were provided by the colony—and there was nothing to worry about. The "home" was a little room, a kitchen or outhouse, large enough for two beds and a table. And since the father was out at night on his post, his bed was taken by his son. But if there was a second child, there was no room for it. Its bed stood outside during the day; and in the night it was somehow jammed in alongside the other two.

Those were nights without sleep for the Jewish mother. If she dozed off, she would start up again, to listen for the whistle signal from her husband, which told her where he was.

The *Shomer* received all of his pay in kind. Every colonist was pledged to contribute so much grain toward his keep. But there were some who dodged their obligation, and in the interval, before the colony council could straighten out the dispute, the *Shomer's* family went on short rations. In our colony, Meschah, we found a pillar of support during bad days in the teacher Entoby. He turned over to us a little stretch of soil close by the school, which the children were not working. This plot the wives of the *Shomrim* turned into a vegetable patch; and what the colonists failed to pay we made up from the soil. We got an excellent harvest of greens, so that we even had some to sell.

Meschah was, for our little group, the last stop after a long life of vagabondage. The *Shomer* organisation had done its work. Wherever it had once entered, only Jewish guards were used. But we did not want to remain professional guards. And so the families Gileadi, Seid, Gad-Kurakin, and four unmarried young men—all of them *Shomrim* in Meschah—resolved to go up into some place in Upper Galilee, to found there a settlement of their own.

Israel Gileadi went out in advance and on his return told us he had spoken with Kalvariski, who was for several decades the representative of the Jewish Colonisation Association for Upper Galilee. Together with the latter he had visited the proposed site, and had also been offered a little budget. We could begin to work. One morning in the month of Tishri (August) in the year 1916, the men saddled their horses—all of our live stock—and rode away to Galilee. The women and children remained behind until the men had found lodgings for them.

Two weeks later we received the news that room had been found for us in the colony of Metulah, which was not far from our stretch of soil. A colonist would come down to Tiberias to meet us and when we arrived in Tiberias the colonist's cart was already waiting for us. From Tiberias to Rosh Pinah there was some sort of a road. But beyond this there was only mud, into which the cart frequently sank to the axle. For by now the winter rains had begun.

On the road, in the valley of the Huleh (the great wild swamp which lies to the north of the Waters of Merom) my little two-year-old child was suddenly seized with convulsions, and not one of us knew what to do. There was a doctor in Metulah, and another in Rosh Pinah, but we were between these points and could not decide which way to turn.

So we stopped the cart and began to rub the child almost

till it bled. But there were some who said that the child
should not be rubbed at all. It should be left in peace.

Arabs came by, inhabitants of the Huleh. One of them
drew close and said to us, indignantly: "Don't you see
that the child is dead? In the name of God! leave it in
peace!" The other Arabs drew closer, gathered round the
child, and repeated, "The child is dead!"

We were a long way from Metulah, and in between there
was not a single Jewish settlement.

And as we stood there in despair, now rubbing the child,
now letting it lie, a cart appeared in the distance, descend-
ing from the Metulah hills. My heart jumped. I was sure
help had come. The cart was in a great hurry, but I threw
myself across its path and made it stop. In it sat a *Ger*—a
Judaising European gentile—a big healthy fellow. I asked
him: "Which is nearer, Metulah or Rosh Pinah?" He said
Metulah was nearer. I begged him to unharness his best
horse, take my baby, and ride as fast as he could to
Metulah. He tried at first to get out of it. But I gave him
one and a half pounds in money—all we could scrape together in our group—and promised him more in Metulah.
He agreed.

I had given my youngest, three-week baby into the arms
of a comrade. The *Ger* rode away before us with the
sick child, and I mounted another horse and followed him.
But he went fast, and soon was lost in the distance.

The road was new to me, and the terror which I felt for
my child confused my sense of direction. It seemed to me
that every tree in the distance was the rider with my child.
I urged the horse along what I thought was the right road,
and the horse, knowing the path better than I, refused to
obey. I became desperate, whipped it, forced it on. And
finally it brought me to the edge of a cliff, and stood there
sorrowfully, as if to say: "Where are you trying to drive
me? Now we'll have to turn back." I gave the horse free
rein after that, and he brought me back again to the right
road. I hardly knew by this time what I was doing, and

I do not know what strength kept me going. But I did go on. And meanwhile I tried to prepare for the worst. I repeated to myself, "The child is dead." Such things had happened to others—why not to me?

I rode into the Arab village of Halsa, and there I asked, "Did a rider pass this way with a baby in his arms?"

Yes, they had seen a rider.

"Is the child alive?"

"We don't know. We only saw it in his arms."

"Which is the road to Metulah?"

"*Dugri!* Straight on!"

And so I rode onward alone. Suddenly, at the top of the hill, among the eucalyptus trees a red roof peeped out, and my heart jumped. Metulah! Yes, I could see the stone houses. I drew up to the first house, jumped off my horse, and ran over to a group of Arabs squatting on the ground.

"Where did the rider with the child go?"

They opened big eyes. "We saw no rider."

"Where do the Jews live?"

"There are no Jews here."

"Isn't this Metulah?"

"No, this is Halta."

"And where is Metulah?"

"*Dugri!*"

My strength was ebbing, and the road among the hills tortured me. But suddenly I met, on the road, some of the comrades from Meschah. Yes, they had seen the rider. The child was alive. But I would not believe them, and I implored them to tell me the truth. They repeated: "The child is alive!"

Then I asked them: "What are you doing here on the road?"

They told me they were hiding from government agents who were looking for men who had run away from military service, and for horses for the army.

"Then you'd better take my horse," I said.

I left the horse with them and ran ahead on foot. I know
the Metulah roads well today, but for the life of me I
cannot remember by which path I came into the village. I
asked the first person I met for the home of the woman
doctor, and rushed in. It was Mrs. Ben Ami, the daughter
of the famous writer, and she recognized me at once, for
we had worked together in the hospital of Zichron Yakob.

"Is the child alive?"

"Alive!" she answered. "It's already called for its dad-
dy. Is it your child, Zipporah?"

"Yes!" I answered, "And where is the father?"

"The soldiers took him away last night. He's in Djaida
now. . ."

That night the cart with the other women came in. I
lived three days with Mrs. Ben Ami, until my child was
well again.

We were quartered in Metulah for a whole year. We
kept all our clothes and foodstuffs in common, but our
lodgings were widely scattered, and so we could not keep
a common kitchen. This was a great drawback in the
work.

Our stretch of soil was in a place called Chamarah, by
the lake Chatzbani, a two hours' remove from Metulah.
The married men worked the soil of Chamarah, and the
unmarried boys worked as guards for the Metulah colonists. In the evening, when the workers returned from the
fields, they took off their shoes and gave them to the
guards; and the guards put them on to wear in the night.
In the morning the guards returned the shoes to the
workers. All that winter not one of the men knew what
it was to draw on a dry pair of shoes.

In order to reach our fields in time, and get substantial
work done, it was necessary to go out with the first glimmer of dawn, and to return by starlight. The wife remained all day long alone with her children. There was
no place to go. There was nowhere to buy anything,
and, if there had been, there was no money.

When the little sack of wheat was brought home, the woman would first sort it, then load it on her back and trudge off to the mill. There she waited some three hours until the slow, old-fashioned millstones had ground the grain into flour. And when she got home at last she had to start looking for fuel to heat up the oven. We would go out into the fields and gather thorns.

There was no water in Metulah. To do our washing we had to go down with our baskets of laundry to the Wady or Gulch of Charad. And then we used to return with the baskets of wet wash on our heads. I would get the feeling that my head was being rammed down between my shoulders. The labor of those years used us up early, and left many of us sick.

When the great day of the first harvest came, we all went out, women and children, old and young. We put up a tent in the middle of the field, and left the children there. One mother remained to look after them, and the other women went out with the men to the mowing.

A terrific plague of mosquitos and other insects tormented us. They seemed to like, more than everything else, the blood of the little ones. In the early morning there was some relief, but evenings the children would return swollen with bites, and raw with rubbing.

There was plenty of sickness, too. The woman doctor had left Metulah, and no one had been sent to replace her. So we had to use the doctor of the Christian Arab village of Darmames, who was much thought of by the colonists of Metulah. It was his practice to listen to his patients only when he was drunk; and he always demanded pay in advance—in money and wine. On top of this, he was his own apothecary, and after the official visit to him as a doctor, one had to go to him for the medicine, too.

There lived with us at that time a certain Yáfah Kurakina-Gad, the daughter of a family of Russian converts to Judaism in Sedjera. She had been brought up in the famous collective of Sedjera. Yafah's little child fell sick, and the women took turns in helping to watch it. During the day Yafah could manage alone, but evenings she was exhausted, and we relieved her.

One night, coming in, I found her in a state of collapse. I told her to go to bed, but she would not, and so we sat together. Early in the morning I went home and sent someone to Darmames for medicine, for the child was in a bad way.

When the medicine was brought, I took it to the sick child. Yafah half sat and half lay on her bed, and the child was on her lap. I began to wake them—but it was only Yafah who responded after long efforts. The child could no longer be awakened. And when Yafah came to herself, and perceived the dead child, she broke into a tempest of weeping, and reproached me for having awakened her. "Would to God," she cried, "you had let me sleep forever with the child!" And I knew well why she longed for death. This was the second child she had lost in this life of vagabondage.

We left Metulah and settled for good in the new place, to which we gave the name of K'far Gileadi. We put up a single barrack, for all purposes. The walls we covered with straw matting, and one half of the interior we divided off into five rooms. In the other half we put the kitchen, the dining room, a section for the children, and a special corner for—God save the mark!—our social life. Outside, against one of the walls, we put up the cowshed, and against the cowshed, we put up the chicken coop. We had no barn. So we hung boxes from the ceiling of the barrack, and this was our "store-room."

In the summer we lived in tents of straw matting and life was easier then.

One woman was busy with the children, another was occupied in the kitchen, and I had my own special job. I was the colony expert in washing the grain. As a matter of fact, quite a little skill was needed for the Chamarah grain, because it was always mixed with red earth (*cham-*

arah means "clay soil" in Arabic) and the washing had to be done down at the lake. An Arab taught me the trick. If you mix the grain with earth, and pour it into a bucket of water, three layers are formed. The bottom layer is earth, the next *taradan* (seeds of wild grass) and the top clean wheat.

The wagon that used to take the workers out in the morning would also take me, with all my paraphernalia and my bags of wheat. All day long I sat alone on the edge of the lake Tayun, and washed the grain, laying it to dry on straw matting. In the evening the wagon came my way again, and took me home with my bundles.

The children would bring me my meals to the lake edge. Their reward was—to be allowed to bathe in the clear waters of the lake and to run around naked afterwards. One day a caravan of camels passed by. The children ran out of the water and began to throw stones at the camels. The Arabs were astounded. What were these strange children doing in this place? White! And alone! And at that moment it was hard to tell which were less civilised—the black Bedouins or our little ones.

When the Arabs began to look around more closely, they saw the tip of a roof projecting over the distant hill; and there, down by the lake, a woman sat alone, washing wheat. Still more astonished, they came over, and asked me whether I was not afraid to sit there alone.

"That's my bodyguard that attacked you," I answered, pointing to the children.

The Arabs broke into laughter.

The laundry and the baking was also my work. Our comrade Yafah was no longer able to help. She lay sick, and she suffered doubly because she was a burden on us. But it was not given to us to carry that precious burden for long. A few months later she died.

Sheikh Abrik   ZIPPORAH SEID.

MY COMING TO PALESTINE

JUST on the day when my dreams seemed about to be realised, and a new life was opening before me, my deepest doubts returned, and I asked myself: "Is this the way of my life?"

I was active in those days in the Zemstvo, or village council, in Russia. An important task had been entrusted to me. I was working for the people whom I knew, whose language and whose ways I had absorbed. For this people I had been trained and educated.

I was the only Jewish girl in the entire Russian village— nor did I forget that fact for a single moment of my life. This world to which I had given myself, and which wrapped me around so closely, was not my own. And yet that doubt haunted me. It pursued me from the village into the city, followed me down the corridors of the University, faced me in the bright-lit theatre and sat opposite me at the writing desk in my beloved study. Was I choosing the right path?

And on an unforgetable night I made my decision. There was a happy crowd in my student's room, comrades of mine, chattering joyously. I was the only one who was not at home there. One by one threads within me were tearing. I could not hear what my comrades were saying. I heard instead the desolate howling of the wolves in the nearby zoo, and something in my heart responded. My life, my whole life has been a mistake till now! The people to whom I have dedicated myself till now is not my own: I am a stranger in its midst. And that other people, my *own* people, is a stranger to me. I know nothing of its life and language. Yes, I know the little tailor, the little shopkeeper—but they are not the people. But among the

Russians I know the stevedores on the dock, the peasants who hunger amid their harvests, the lean, staring women and children who stream out evenings from the factory when the bell rings. These are the masses. But where are the masses of my own people? I must begin again, from the very beginning.

One by one my guests leave, wondering at my silence and my sadness, for this is not my wont. When they are gone, I too step outside, and through the starlit night I still hear, but more clearly than before, the melancholy howling of the wolves. A shiver goes through me. I cannot go on like this.

That night I packed my things, and in the morning left by the first boat for my parents' home in the village.

*   *   *

The warm days of autumn came, and it was strange to be at home instead of in the big city. The folks look at me wonderingly. For hours I wander along the banks of the Dnieper, sunk in thought, and feel the broad autumn winds on my cheeks and hair. On rainy days I stay at home, and pore helplessly over my father's stock of Hebrew books, row upon row of them in a language which I cannot understand. And yet it becomes clear to me that in these books lies the key to my life. The thought ripens in me. I must learn the language of my people—for there is no other way of coming close to them. The months go by and still I wander on the banks of the Dnieper. The sun warms me no longer. A cold wind blows, carrying the first snowflakes, and the beginnings of the winter sleep settle like a blanket on the life of the village. And still I am undecided. I do not know where to begin.

January comes. The village dozes under the thick snow. The family has gone to a neighboring village, and I am at home alone. I sit fingering my father's letters. I know that most of them are from Palestine or about Palestine, but I cannot read a single word. . . Then suddenly I come across a letter in Russian, from Vladimir Tiomkin, the

Zionist leader. I remember now that my father had told me about this letter long ago—but in those days it had all been alien to me. But now every word of that letter is like a seed in ploughed soil. A stronger passion wakes in me with every line, and then suddenly, like a thunderbolt, comes the unalterable resolution: there, in Palestine, are the workers of my people! I will go to them, and become one of them. Other thoughts rise, attempt to disturb me, but they are carried away as by a strong wind. I wrap myself up, leave the house, and go down once more to the old friend whose wordless counsel I have always depended on, Grandfather Dnieper. From bank to bank the river is one iron sheet: but underneath I feel the waters moving stormily. I am alone in the white wilderness, and unashamed I shout at the top of my voice: "I am going to Palestine!"

* * *

The ship drives through the storm, and a cold, wet mist clings to the waters and to the ship. My fellow passengers cower together for warmth, but in me there is only a fierce jubilation. I stand alone on the deck, untouched by the cold and darkness. I know nothing of the land I am going to, and there is not a single person there I have ever met. I only know that there are men and women working for their people, and I belong to them.

My fellow-passengers to Palestine were two or three wrinkled greybeards going to spend their last years in the Holy Land, and a woman with a child. The little boy could sing Hebrew songs; and I would sit with him in a corner and listen to his thin, childish treble piping the songs of our country.

Any Palestinian port was the same to me; so I landed at Haifa with the mother and her boy, and went with them to a hotel. I was trusting to Providence .... Someone would surely turn up who would want to know what I was doing here in Palestine. And if it was the right kind of person, then I would know that I had found my path.

I sat at the table in the dining-room and listened to the conversation. And the first one to come up to me was a young man with a long beard which made him look much older than he was. He came up with his hands in his pockets, and his head slightly on one side, and before he spoke a word I had already taken a liking to his clever, laughing eyes. I knew I could trust his advice.

Early the next morning I had changed from my heavy winter clothes into a light summer dress, and, filled with hope, set out with B. for the colony Merchaviah.

Sixteen years have passed since that morning. What was then strange and incomprehensible has now become intimate and simple. Illusions were born and died. There have been hopes which proved false, and others which have been fulfilled; men and women have been close to me, and have drifted away. But as long as I live I will remember those eyes which shone on me in my loneliness with so much brotherly love and understanding.

I am in the *kvutzah* of Deganiah, by the Jordan. Today for the first time, I am permitted to bake the bread on my own responsibility. "Bread for fifty people!" I say to myself, and alternately I swell up with pride and shrink with terror. How does a little creature like myself come to undertake this tremendous task, and face a gigantic oven full of loaves? Yes, I know the theory of it perfectly. B., the skilful baker, has taught me everything. She told me exactly how long to knead the dough; she told me when to add the water, and was very emphatic about adding only a little at a time.

She gives me her instructions, and goes out. And now I must convert theory into practice. A little time passes and my hands begin to tremble with exhaustion. The fingers won't obey orders. I put all my strength into it—but the flour will not turn into dough. I know I oughtn't to do it, but I add more water, and the flour turns into a sticky, sloppy mess. I can't pull my hands out without dragging everything along. I twist them, rub them—no use! My back aches, I am tortured by thirst, the flies settle on my face and I can't drive them away. They crawl over my forehead, into my eyes and mouth. "Bread for fifty people!" I repeat to myself, and attack the mess of flour and water again. I feel all my strength running out of me. I stand on one foot, then on the other. I try to think of other things, but I am haunted by one thought: I want to add more water. M. passes by and looks at me with pitying eyes.

And now—at last, the first good signs. Something like dough begins to emerge. It grows smoother and less clinging, and I can free my hands. I can add water, drink a little myself, and wipe the sweat off my face. The torture changes to pleasure. A stone has fallen from my heart, or I feel as if I had just thrown off my winter mantle and run out with the first sign of spring, over the green meadows.

It seems to me that only yesterday I was a thing torn by doubts and hesitations. In the noisy city, in the great library, in the museum, in the classes, the question would suddenly confront me: Why are you doing these things? Who needs you? Can't they do without you and people like you? And in such moments a paralysing apathy would creep over me; I wanted to see no one, speak with no one. But now? My comrades are out in the field, mowing the harvest which we have sown. Close by I hear the mill grinding out grain. And the flour from the mill comes straight to me, and I bake the bread for all of us. Bread is surely needed.

Nahalal   DEBORAH DAYAN.

A KVUTZAH OF SHEPHERDS

IN THE first year of the war there was a severe crisis in Palestine, and because of the difficulties of communication the *Histadruth,* the Jewish Workers' Federation, was split into two sections, with separate executive committees, one for Judaea and one for Galilee. Outside of the four *kvutzoth* or communes (Deganiah, Kinereth, Merchaviah and Tel Adas which were settled on the land of the Jewish National Fund and were sure of work and bread) there were some hundred workers in Galilee, all unemployed. The Committee decided, then, that every worker who had parents or relatives in Judæa, and who could find food and shelter there, should leave Galilee. For those who had to remain work was found drying the swamps of the Jordan and clearing the stones off the hills of Kinereth. The swamps, as it happened, needed to be dried, for they were a source of sickness; but we felt that the National Fund was undertaking this only for our sake, and the thought depressed us.

It was known in Galilee that I had a sister in Judæa who could take me in; but I had made up my mind to starve rather than leave Kinereth.

On the first day of the new arrangement I went out with comrades I had met before to carry stones off the hills. We worked in groups of three, with two baskets to a group for carrying away the stones. In my little group was A. D Gordon, but I did not know him and had not even heard his name. I only saw an old man who was drawn toward young people, and who labored cheerfully with them, unbowed in body or spirit by his years. And when, on that first day, I felt myself collapsing under the unwonted labor; and under the fierce heat of the Kinereth sun (it was Tamuz then—August) he cheered me and laughed and repeated (how many have heard him say it!) : "Look at me, I am an old man, and I don't lose heart. And you are young and you despair on the first day. Look! Let me show you how to carry a basket full of stones without getting tired."

Three months later the Federation of Labor undertook the work on the Tiberias road. The Government had ordered the colonists of Galilee to prepare gravel, and the colonists turned over the work to the Federation. It was a contract job and so the first group went out for a week to break stones and to determine at the same time what the price should be. It was with the utmost difficulty that I, a woman, could persuade the comrades to take me along. There were all sorts of objections. The work was too much for a girl; it wasn't nice for a Jewish girl to be working on the open road. There was even one comrade who believed that it would be a national crime! But I and another girl stuck it out for the first week and, in spite of renewed objections, stayed on. At the end of the first month there was a whole group of women at work on the road.

The work came to an end, and I determined to link up with the shepherds who were employed on the herds of the Galilee colonists. These shepherds had an idea all their own. They were going to stay long enough with the colonists to learn the trade and after that they would turn Bedouin, get sheep and cattle of their own and live a wandering life in the fields of Palestine. The idea caught my fancy, and I joined the group. Here again we worked in threes: two shepherds and myself in one group; they looked after the flocks and I was, so to speak, the "housekeeper."

We lived in a room without doors or windowpanes. There was no gasolene for the lamp; and, if there had been, we couldn't have used it, because of the wind which always blew through the hut. The "pay" of the shepherds was not enough to keep them. They were paid in kind—and at that the pay of one was regularly withheld as a possible forfeit against loss of cattle.

We struggled through half the winter starving much of

the time. My comrades would go out with the herds into the hills, and take with them, as their day's ration, a piece of dry bread. Before they left they drank several cups of hot tea with sugar, to warm themselves. I would get up early to boil the water; then I would go out and drive the herds together, so that they should not wander over the sown fields of the colonists.

A morning came when there was no bread in the hut, and my comrades went out to the herds without their ration. I cannot forget that day. A fierce rain was driving across the country, and my comrades went to the top of the hill to look for pasture. But as they came downward with the flocks, three of the cows fell into a huge hole and were killed. Hungry, raging, and wet to the skin, they came "home"—and there was not a piece of bread for them. I was unable to get out of bed. They asked nothing of me, nor I of them. We only looked at each other.

At last one of them got up, went down to a colonist, and returned with a loaf of bread fresh from the oven. We tore the warm bread into three parts, and swallowed it—our meal for the day.

And when the year came to an end, we had a trial on our hands. We had not only not received our pay—we were supposed to make good the lost animals. The worst that could happen did happen: we were fired.

Ain Charod   REBECCA DANITH.

IN THE WAR YEARS

I

"EXCUSE me, Gottlieb, aren't you a member of the Workers' Council? I was told to apply to you for work. I want to start tomorrow morning."

"There's no ladies' work."

"I don't want 'ladies' work'. I'll do any kind. They told me workers are needed here; that's why I came."

"I don't know. The colonists don't want girls."

"But you're making a mistake. I'm not looking for girls' work. Are you afraid I won't make good? Give me a chance. If I don't get through the regulation amount, take it off my pay."

"I'll see. Come in tomorrow."

Six months later, before the rains set in, Gottlieb said to me: "You know that the heavy work is over. We've got to start in making the 'saucers'—the holes round the trees to catch the rain water. If you like, you can start after Saturday."

We began on Sunday. The sky was grey, the air heavy with moisture. The rain seemed to be suspended about us, and the "saucers" had to be dug in a hurry. Eighteen of us worked in one vineyard, systematically, silently, rhythmically. The spades swung up and down together and the rain seemed to be holding back specially for us. We had passed over into the second half of the vineyard, and had come close to the ploughed land beyond, with its wild thorns and grasses. And now the air could no longer contain its burden. The first big drops fell—and in a few minutes the flood was all about us. We picked up our spades and dashed back to the colony, wet to the skin and happy.

Saturday morning. The rain beats down steadily. In the little barrack which is our kitchen the workers stand at the windows, watch the swelling pools outside, and fall into thought. The rain seeps in through the windows, and yellow streaks of water crawl down over the white walls. The rain is so heavy that it may wash away the last rows of trees at the other end of the vineyard on the downward slope. The owner is at some distance, in the next colony. If he waits till the rain lets up, it may be too late, and the trees will be torn up by the roots. Suddenly I put on my rainproof (my good and clever mother! only she could have remembered to make me take a rainproof along) pick up my spade and run through the vineyard. The rain had in fact washed away a whole row of shoots. I shovel the earth together swiftly and plant the shoots firmly again. The rain whips my face and holds up the work; the sloppy earth clings to the spade. Two hours work is enough, and the shoots are saved.

Winter in the kitchen. It's time to clear the tables and wash up the breakfast things. We had tea with raisins instead of sugar, and a salad of oranges with spring onions dipped in oil: two oranges to a person. It's wartime, and there's no exportation; so for a few piastres we can buy oranges enough for all the workers. Now we have to sort the beans and peas and soak them, and prepare the meal before the boys come back from the vineyards. Before nine in the morning we have to go out and gather stocks of *inzhil*—a sort of wild grass—and spread it round the north side of our neighbor's oven. By tomorrow the *inzhil* will be dry enough to serve as fuel, and then we can bake. We have about enough bread to last us till then. And now it's time to put the pots on the stove constructed of a few cans. Afterwards comes the evening meal, flat cakes which we baked together with the bread; the cakes are dipped in oil and prepared with lots of garlic. They are eaten with the pea soup.

Spring. We are filling up the "saucers" round the trees.
Four men are at work in the vineyard: a Yemenite, a
Galician and two Russians. They dig along the length of
the vineyard, two rows at a time; and every five minutes
they pause and rest. The four men have no language in
common; the Yemenite understands Hebrew, but he speaks
Arabic; the Galician understands Hebrew and Arabic but
speaks Yiddish. The Russians know only Russian.

When the work first began, the men wanted to help the
girl finish her rows; but it soon became clear that the one
who needed help was the Russian boy, because he was
behind. On the way back home one of the boys wants to
relieve the girl of her spade. And suddenly it occurs to
him that when you are going home after a day's heavy work
you don't feel the spade on your shoulder. The hand which
was half stretched toward the girl drops again.

II

"Don't go to Samaria"—so I was told. "You don't need
it at all. There's plenty of work here in Petach Tikvah.
Your *kvutzah* is occupied every day. And the colonist P.
came into the Council office yesterday and said he would
give you a steady job in his orchard. You won't have to do
heavy work; you'll be overseer, and you'll have an Arab
boy as assistant."

And while I was being told this, the wild man M.
growled: "What's the sense of talking to her? She'll listen
—and then she'll do exactly the opposite."

Rather than submit to *suchra* (forced labor) in Beersheba
and in other places which were far from Jewish settlements
and were filled with infectious diseases, many of our workers left for Samaria to chop down eucalyptus trees for the
government. In exchange they got food and liberation from
the military service. When women workers were asked
for, to keep house in Samaria, I reported. There were plenty
of others to do my work in Petach Tikvah . . . .

There were three girls in the group which clambered on to the carts which carried wheat from Galilee to Judæa. At Tul Kerem the road divides, one branch leads to Galilee, the other to Samaria; and there we had to get out and wait for a chance conveyance.

The railway was being used in those days exclusively by the military, and so we waited at Tul Kerem. We waited till our patience gave out, and finally we slung our packs on our shoulders and went ahead on foot. The packs were nearly as long as ourselves—and much broader. They contained our bedding, our laundry, our clothes, and our books. The weight was bad enough; but much worse was the fact that they didn't sit right. The sand was almost as yielding as water, and every footstep was a separate achievement. At last a cart came along, carrying tree trunks. We flung the packs on board, and jumped in after. Life suddenly became tolerable again. In two hours' time we were in Chedera.

Familiar faces in the workers' home. There's Miriam K. standing over a tubful of wash. I watch her enviously; she works so neatly and effortlessly. Where did she get the trick? Laundry! What a back-breaking torture that was for me, and how long it took me to learn!

On the veranda another familiar face—A., who is something of a public busybody.

"The Central Office sent you?" he asks. "But we don't need new workers. Who told them to send you?"

That was our official reception . . . .

Late afternoon drew on. The two girls who had come along with me collapsed from weariness. But I found a young fellow who was returning that evening to the commune of Hefzibah and I went with him—perhaps there would be work. There was no road—only a wilderness of sand. It was here that I got my first glimpse of the *djamus*, the Palestinian buffalo. It was evening when we arrived at Hefzibah. My head ached, and I wanted to lie down. Some of the comrades tried to persuade me to eat something, but I only wanted to lie down. They took my temperature—but they did not tell me till next morning that I had nearly a hundred and six.

This was my first attack of fever—my betrothal to Palestine. At Chedera I had already seen one of the girls lying on the floor with a compress round her head—and in the next room, another. It looked like part of a local custom.

We began to work, some of us in the orchards of the Agudath Netaim, the planter's association—and some in Hefzibah. We used to work immediately before and after the attacks of fever. Soon the following message came from Sarah Lishansky, who was at that time a nurse in Karkur: "You've got a girl down there, among the workers who came from Judæa. Her name is Judith and she has two long braids down her back. Send her up here, and if she won't come, drag her by the braids." I didn't wait to be dragged. When I arrived I was shoved at once into the kitchen, and I knew that there was no getting away from this place, because there was no other girl to do the work.

We used to get up at three in the morning, when the threshing machine sent its first melancholy whistle over the grey Karkur fields. We went into the kitchen, an old Arab hut; behind the hut was the well, and opposite was the vegetable patch. We worked and suffered. At ten o'clock the fever would increase suddenly; our limbs trembled, heads ached, and everything fell out of our hands. Twelve o'clock, and it is impossible to go on. I lie down on the bench in the kitchen and wait till the fit passes. Then I get up and work on.

Shortly after my arrival in Karkur I made my first acquaintance with a scorpion.

Work was over and we sat outside, waiting for the carts which were returning from Galilee; we knew that our boys would not want to spend the night in the desolate Wady

Arah. Waiting for them, we passed the time chatting and singing.

D. calls out to me, "Judith! Come over here, there's a clean place to sit down."

I crossed over, and sat down—and leapt wildly to my feet. It was as if the big toe of my right foot had been shoved against a burning coal.

The comrades think it a bit of a joke. "That's D. all over," they say. "When he does get a girl to sit down next to him, she's got to be bitten by a scorpion."

D. is terrified. He almost bursts into tears. "How did it happen?" he keeps on stammering. My foot seems to be steeped in a white fire. I must have trodden on the scorpion, it jabbed me so fiercely—a full shot of poison. Already Sarah is working over me. She rubs the foot with boiling water, and the new pain drives out the old.

All night long, as if to make my pain absolutely intolerable, someone keeps disturbing me by shouting angrily: "What's happened there?" But in the morning I am told that this someone was myself. I had been yelling at the top of my voice till three o'clock. I deny it resolutely—I am always so patient.

And this too passes.

The nakedness of the wide fields lies like a burden on the soul. There is not a single full tree to rest the eye. I long once more for the green places of Judæa, for the shadows, for the little wood, for the shrubs of a vineyard and an orchard of orange trees. Only far away, on the edge of Karkur, a meagre line of eucalyptuses stretches through the desolation. I cannot bear the loneliness of those trees. Sometimes I feel as if I could rush out there with my spade, and dig and dig, and cover the earth with green. And sometimes I feel that even the sun is weary of shining on this barrenness, and longs for something living on which to pour out its warmth and affection.

Ain Charod   JUDITH EDELMAN.

I BECOME A WORKER

I

Two days I waited for my sister Hemdah to take me down to the workers' club. But she never had the time. And at last I decided to go there alone.

A group of workers stood outside the building, and as I drew up, not knowing a soul there, they looked me over curiously, and began to talk about me in friendly mockery:

"Who's this? Pretty, isn't she?"

"And doesn't she know it! Look at the way she holds her head."

I went up boldly and answered: "Suppose I am pretty? What's wrong with that?"

Two young fellows stood apart, looking more impudent than the others. One of them called out: "We can see from your clothes you aren't a worker." I answered in the same tone: "What have my clothes got to do with it? Here— is this the hand of a worker?"

There was a shout of laughter, and voices:

"That's a worker's hand. Big and hefty. Say, how old are you?"

I answered: "I have a friend and she's married."

"And what about you?"

"If you'll be nice boys, I'll marry too."

At this point my nerve broke down. I blushed and began to stammer. This was my introduction to the club.

When I went inside I felt a strange chill of disappointment. The whitewash was peeling from the walls. The tables were small, without covers. At one table sat some workers drinking soup. The waiter came up to one of them, and said sharply: "Listen, you! You've taken two plates of soup and you've given me only one ticket. Where's the second?"

This was beyond me. What were tickets needed for? Didn't they just put the soup on the table and let people eat whatever they wanted?

Someone explained to me: "Every plate has to be paid for separately. You don't think a kitchen can be conducted without some sort of account, do you?"

"But I didn't think you've got to check up on each man, how much he eats."

No, no, this was not what I had expected and I felt a depression coming over me.

The two laughing boys who had been standing outside came up to me.

"Well, how do you like our club?" And without waiting for an answer one of them added: "I suppose you expected a great big hall, with lots of gold-framed pictures on the wall."

I answered frankly: "I didn't quite expect gold frames. Only I thought the place would be simple in another kind of way."

"Well, what way?"

"I did expect a big room. And I also expected big long tables. I don't like little tables, it's too much like a saloon. A big table is homier and friendlier—it draws people together. And why can't you have a white table-cloth on the tables? And why can't you have pictures on the walls—the first pioneers who came on the soil here?"

"Why the pioneers on the soil?"

I answered: "Because we Jews have plenty of city workers everywhere, and there's nothing new in that."

"And what else did you expect?'

"You could have had a few flowerpots in the corners. And if you want to know something more—I thought that the food would be handed out by girls in white pinafores."

"Why don't you come into the club and fix things the way you want?"

"I don't want to work in the kitchen. I want to join a *kvutzah*. I want to learn to work."

"They won't take you into a *kvutzah*. The *kvutzoth* aren't for young girls like you. Besides, you can't speak Hebrew. Forget the *kvutzah*—it's just a dream."

"It's not a dream," I answered proudly. "My brother has friends in a *kvutzah,* and they'll take me in."

"You have a brother here?"

"Yes, and a sister, too."

"Well, well. And who are they?"

"You know them, I think. Their names are Ezra and Hemdah."

"What? Hemdah is your sister? You don't look a bit like her. Listen, if your brother vouches for you, they may let you in. But you might as well know that's just pull."

"No it isn't. My brother is known over there, and he says they can use me. And I hope to start work soon."

"But what do you want a *kvutzah* for?" they started again. "Why don't you join us? We need a girl in the kitchen just now."

"No, I'm going to wait. I want to go to a *kvutzah* if I can."

When I went out of the club that evening the two boys went out after me, and for a little while I caught part of their conversation. . . They were wondering whether I would ever become a real worker.

II

I DIDN'T return to the club. I could not understand the lectures, and I could not sing. There was dancing—but something strange had happened to me. There was a time when I was known as "the dancer." But that was long ago—on the other side. And when I refused to dance at the wedding of my friend, over there, everyone was astonished. But even then it had lost its appeal; my body sought another rhythm now, other motions than those that are made to musical measures.

Two long weeks passed, and no answer came from the *kvutzah*. I grew uneasy, and wondered at the reason. Was it true that it was all a matter of pull? Were they ashamed to answer "No" just because my brother had applied for me? Often, in the street, the two young men I had met at the club passed me by. They smoothed down their masses of hair, greeted me with "*Shalom,*" but did not stop to speak to me. What was going to happen with me? Would I have to work in the club after all?

The thought repelled me. I could not picture myself asking a worker for his "ticket." My brother and sister did not worry. When I complained about my idleness they laughed: "Don't worry. You'll get work all right."

At the end of the two weeks my brother came in one evening and found me in tears. He was startled.

"What's the matter?"

"I don't understand you," I sobbed. "I'm here two weeks, I can't get into a *kvutzah,* and you take it so calmly —as if I'd come here just so."

My brother looked relieved.

"Is that all? I thought something was really the matter. If that's all you want, well, I've got an answer from the *kvutzah*. They ask you to come."

"Read me the letter."

"They say that one of the girls is sick, and there's no one to work in the kitchen. They want you to take the train tomorrow afternoon and at three o'clock they'll meet you at the station."

"Kitchen?" I stammered. "I don't know how to cook. What am I going to do there?"

But this was no time to turn back. I did not sleep that night. At five in the morning I was already up. My sister heard me, and she asked me: "What are you getting up so early for?"

"I want to pack my things over," I said. "I'm ashamed to land there with all this baggage—like a bride getting ready for her wedding. I want to leave out my holiday clothes, and I want to take just a little underwear with me."

"Wait," my sister said. "Don't close up the basket till I've been to the village. I want to give you some money to pack in, just in case."

"In case of what?" I asked. "Do you think I'm going to keep money tied up over there, in the *kvutzah?* You're just making fun of me—I suppose you think I don't know what a *kvutzah* is. I know there's no such thing as 'yours' and 'mine' in a *kvutzah*." ·

"Well, well," my sister said, ironically. "Even in a *kvutzah* they have 'mine' and 'not-mine.' But I know it's no use arguing with you."

Very hastily I prepared my basket. Then I made a separate bundle of my bedding. My sister watched me in astonishment.

"What are you making two separate bundles for?"

"I want to see whether I can carry them myself to the station."

"But, listen," my sister said, patiently. "I've ordered a porter to come to the house."

"All right," I said. "He'll carry the basket and I'll carry the bundle. I'm not going to follow him with nothing in my hands, like a countess."

At eleven o'clock that morning I was down at the station. My brother and sister argued whether I ought to travel alone or not. But Ezra said finally that there was nothing to be afraid of. Besides, now that I was going out into the world, it was better for me to learn independence. I agreed with him—but I turned away so that no one could see the tears in my eyes. Because, after all— suppose no one were to be at the station at the other end?

III

In the train a woman came up to me and said: "I saw a Jewish face, so I had to come and speak to you. There are only Arabs on the train. Where are you going?"

I wiped away the tears quickly and said: "To a *kvutzah*."

"A *kvutzah*? What is that?"

"It's a kind of group," I said, "where everyone works like everyone else, and they all live together."

"What do you mean, 'they all live together'?"

"Well, they all eat in one kitchen, and they all work together."

"Eating and working together—does that mean living together?"

I began to see that neither this woman nor I knew very clearly what a *kvutzah* was.

"And why must you go and work?" she asked me. "Your parents aren't dead, God forbid?'

"No."

The woman was silent awhile. Then she began again:

"You don't look like an ordinary girl to me. I suppose you've been to school. Why can't you be a teacher, or a nurse?"

"I want to work."

"You want to work? Good luck to you. I suppose you're from Russia. My daughter in Jaffa told me that Jews are coming from Russia these days, and building themselves houses on the sands. Some of them have nice clothes, but won't wear them; instead of hats they wear Arab *kefias,* and they work on the land. Good luck to them, too. Maybe they'll put an end to the famine."

I remembered now the day I left home, and my mother's parting words: "God be with you, my child. Work! But you are only a child; don't take on more than you can carry, and don't despise what the world says."

I had always listened to my mother, but I could not

understand what those words meant: "Don't despise what the world says." The world says many things. The world says that money is important. If I had taken along what Hemdah wanted to give me, I would not have to worry now. If there was no one at the station to meet me, I could continue with this woman as far as Jerusalem, and there I could write my brother Ezra to come and fetch me. But what would I do now, without a piastre in my pocket?

Just before my station the conductor comes around, and takes my ticket from me. My heart begins to beat fast. I try to behave calmly. I straighten out my two braids, and smooth out my belt. As the train rolls in, I lean out of the window. The long stretch is as empty as a wilderness. Finally I see a little hut under some eucalyptus trees. Near the hut is a group of Arabs, and when I look closely I see among them a tall, dark boy wearing a white shirt, and carrying a whip in his hand.

When the train stops, the tall boy with the whip is already at my window.

I shout: "Is there a Jew here?"

"Are you Amunah?'

"Yes."

"My name's Abraham. I'm a comrade in the *kvutzah,* and I was sent down to meet you. Let me take your things."

"Not all of them, please."

"Why, what's the matter? You'll get dirty and you'll tear your dress. Here, you hold my whip. I'll take the basket, then I'll come back for the bundle."

"Please, *I'll* carry the bundle."

The boy laughed out loud, and stopped arguing with me. Basket and bundle were packed into the middle of the cart. The boy examined the arrangement thoughtfully, and said: "Well, that won't upset." It was a real task to climb into the cart, for my dress was too tight. He watched

me with great solicitude, and felt guilty when something
ripped.

We hardly spoke along the journey. All his attention
was given to the driving. He watched every stone, every
rut, and managed the mules with the utmost care. Before
every bump he warned me anxiously to hold tight.

IV

WHEN we crawled into the yard, not a soul was visible.
Abraham called out: "Before long it'll be easier to steal
things here by day than by night. At night we have the
guard, but during the day there's no one around." Then
he added, half solicitously, half sarcastically: "I suppose
that Shachar, the Guardian of Israel, is sitting all the time
at Hasidah's bedside. . .

Then he turned to me, and his face beamed: "And we
didn't have an upset!"

I went into the house with beating heart. The first to
meet us was Shachar himself. He stood there, book in
hand, and said, in amazement: "When did you get here?
I didn't hear the creaking of the cart." Then he introduced
himself. "My name's Shachar, one of the comrades in the
kvutzah. He looked at me out of watery, colorless eyes,
and added: "I suppose you're tired. That road would tire
out anybody."

"No," I answered, "In fact, I enjoyed the ride."

"Enjoyed it?" he repeated. He turned to Abraham.
"And didn't the cart upset?"

Abraham seemed hurt. "You talk as if I did nothing but
upset carts. You're a first-class watchman, I must say.
Here we come riding into the yard and you don't even
hear us."

Angrily Shachar answered: "No, I didn't hear you. I
had to change the compress for Hasidah, and I sat with
her a while."

"All right, then," Abraham said. "But now will you tell me where the grain measure is? I don't know when you fellows will learn to leave it where it ought to be. I've got to feed the mules. Will you look after that, Shachar? I'm the cook today, and I've got to get supper ready."

"I can't. I've got to be near Hasidah." And then Abraham told me to follow him, so that Hasidah could have a look at me. When we got into the room, he asked the girl who was lying down whether she wanted the cold compress changed. Then he added: "Here's the new comrade."

Hasidah opened her eyes and, without greeting, she said: "Oh, she's too young, too young. Have you been long in Jaffa?"

"Two weeks," I answered.

"Then why didn't you cut your braids off? They'll be ruined here, anyway."

"Why should I cut them off? I asked, startled. "My sister has even longer ones, and she manages all right."

"Your sister doesn't work in the field," she answered. "If you want to work you'll have to cut those braids off."

"Of course I want to work. I'll cut my braids off if I have to."

"And look at your dress. It's ripped. That isn't the kind of dress to come to work in."

"That's nothing," I said, wretchedly. "I've got other dresses."

She made a motion to Shachar to change the compress, and then she closed her eyes. I went away from this reception with my heart in my shoes. "I'll go to Abraham," I thought. "I feel better near him."

I found him in the kitchen. "Come in," he said, cheerfully. "You'll see what kind of a cook I am. Can you cook?"

"No."

"Doesn't matter. I'll teach you. I'll teach you Hebrew, too."

"Honest?"

"Can you ride a horse?"

"No. I've never been on one."

"You'll learn that, too. We'll go out riding in the fields."

"Can I help you to get supper ready?"

"No, it's all right. I'll be through soon. If you like, you can clean the lamp glass. It hasn't been wiped since Hasidah fell sick."

He gave me a rag, and I, not noticing there was a button in the holder, smashed the glass. . .

Abraham started. "Hey, what's that? What are we going to do now?"

I didn't know the extent of the catastrophe, but I guessed it from his tone. I remained standing in a sort of paralysis.

After an awful silence, he began to console me. "Oh, well, we'll get another one tomorrow. But you don't know what a lamp chimney means in a village like this. We've had to sit in the dark for a whole week, sometimes, before we could lay our hands on one of those treasures. Without one you can't do a thing nights—not even read the newspaper."

In the evening they began to return from the fields. The first man in was Aaron, and his first words were, "Well, is the new girl here?"

"Yes."

"Why is it dark? Why don't you light the lamp?"

"Can't. The new girl's already broken the glass."

"She has? That's not so good. Tell me, is she pretty at least?"

"Oh, be quiet. I don't know."

Aaron dashed off, and came back in a moment with the stable lantern, and set it on the table. He looked me over, and then said with a smile, to Abraham: "You've nothing to be angry about."

Somebody else came in, grumbling: "What's the idea of taking the lantern out of the stable? I nearly knocked one of my eyes out."

"Don't get excited. I took it. I wanted to see our new comrade, and there's no lamp. So I took the lantern."

"Was it worth while, at least?"

"I didn't get a good look, but I guess it was."

v

IN THE morning Abraham remained behind to show me my work. The first thing he asked me was whether I could cut onions into small pieces. When I said I could, he went for two barrels of water, and in the meantime told me to keep an eye on the oil which was standing over the fire; I was to take it off as soon as it had warmed up—but I was to be very careful about it, because if the oil became too hot the onions would burn when thrown in. He went out, and I remained alone in the kitchen. I was eager to do my best—but in taking off the oil, I slopped half of it on the floor. A feeling of despair came over me. In the evening my great skill was the subject of wide discussion. They asked Abraham whether he would go on teaching me how to cook. He answered angrily: "What makes you all so impatient? Were you born workers? Did you find it so easy to learn?"

The next day things went smoothly. I peeled onions; I washed the bread-box; I did everything according to Abraham's instructions and he was happy. "They'll have nothing to grumble about today. Now put the milk on the stove, and for God's sake, watch it closely, and don't let it run over, I've got to get more water, or there'll be no tea for dinner."

"I'll be careful," I said.

I stand watching the milk closely, waiting for the first sign of the rise. And suddenly I hear Hasidah's voice: "Amunah, bring me a glass of water. I don't feel well." I run in, give her water, straighten out the cushions, and ask anxiously: "Is that better?" But suddenly she makes a face, and asks abruptly: "Did you leave the milk on the stove? What's the matter with you?" I dash back. Too late! The milk is running down the sides of the pot, and streaming on to the floor. My heart dies in me. What's going to happen now? How will they be able to eat the gruel? They'll be hungry—and all on my account. But what could I do? Shouldn't I have given the sick woman a glass of water?

When Abraham came in, he turned pale. "Again?" he said.

In an instant he had fixed everything, added coals and thrown salt on the stove.

"If you'd at least thrown salt on. The smoke is terrible."

"Thrown salt on what?"

"On the stove, so as to keep the smoke down. I forgot to tell you. I didn't expect this to happen."

He put water on for tea, and went into Hasidah's room. I wiped the milk off the floor, and began to sweep the room. A cry came from Hasidah: "Shut that door. I'm choking with the dust and smoke."

Abraham came in: "Why don't you sprinkle water on the floor before sweeping? You're not like a girl at all. . . Don't you even know how to sweep?"

"I know how to sweep. I didn't want to use water because you've got to bring it such a way, and perhaps all of it is needed. And I was frightened to ask you because you looked so angry before."

"Don't you think I ought to be?"

VI

THAT evening I was again the subject of discussion. Again they asked Abraham: "Well, are you still going to teach her?"

Abraham lost his temper. "Why do you pick on me? Am I responsible? Did I bring her here?"

Shachar added: "I talked with Hasidah. She said we

ought to take her out of the kitchen—we can't stand all that damage. Anyway, she can do some washing. Since Hasidah fell sick no washing's been done, and we haven't a clean thing to put on for the work."

I am asked if I can wash clothes. Sure! I am filled with joy: here's something I can do, at last.

When I got up early next morning, there were already two barrels of water at hand, brought by Abraham. He showed me the three stones which served as stove, and the heap of thorns which served as fuel. Following Abraham's advice, I poured a lot of washing soda into the hot water, and rubbed the clothes well. But when I got to the dark clothes, I couldn't rub any more, because there was no more skin on my hands. I could neither wash the clothes nor wring them out. Miserable, ashamed, humiliated at my helplessness, I began to cry. It was the first time in my life that things were going against me. And when Abraham came up, I showed him my hands.

He smiled. "You're a real worker," he said, "there's no getting away from that. Leave the clothes in the boiler, with water. You'll finish tomorrow."

I took down the wash, which was dry by now, and went into Hasidah's room. The village nurse was there. As I came in, I heard her say:

"Now that you've got a new girl, things'll be easier for you."

"She's not much of a help," Hasidah said. "We've made an unlucky choice. She wants to work, but she doesn't know how. And she's too childish for a *kvutzah*."

The nurse asked me to sew two towels together, and make a compress.

"I can't," I said. "My hands are all raw, and I can't straighten my fingers out."

"Let me see. How did you get them that way?"

"From the wash."

There was a frightened look on her face. "Don't let any water come on your hands for the next few days."

"How can I do that? There's a tubful of laundry outside."

Hasidah smiled. "That's my help. There's something
queer about her. The first thing she told me was that she
has a lot of clothes, and her sister has even longer braids
than she."

And after a pause she added: "It looks as though a
long time will have to pass before we have the right kind
of people coming to the country."

VII

THOSE three days without work were misery. Meanwhile Hasidah got up from her bed, and with her about
the house things improved, and the mood improved too.
We had to do the baking now. Hasidah said: "If your
hands get better I'll give you the kneading to do." I would
work under her direction, and she would attend to the
cooking, because sowing time had come and Abraham
could no longer remain at home. Mornings there was a
lively feeling of work in the air, and everyone was up with
the dawn.

"Amunah, today you'll do the kneading. Are your
hands all right?"

I answered resolutely, "Yes." I put a white kerchief
round my head, and took a new apron out of my basket,
one that I had not yet worn in the country. I was preparing as if for a ritual.

"I'm ready, Hasidah."

She looked me over. "White!" she exclaimed. "From
head to foot, like a nurse at the operating table." And
when she gave me flour and water, and told me to start
kneading, I was as excited as if I were undergoing rather
than watching an operation. I kneaded away lustily. From
time to time the dough clung to my hands and was flecked
with blood from my half-healed flesh. Without saying a
word I would detach the bloodstained pieces of dough, and

throw them on the floor. Hasidah called out to me: "Be careful no flies get into the bread."

When the dough was kneaded to her satisfaction, she said: "We've got to heat the oven now."

"I'm frightened. I know I'll spoil something."

"Don't be frightened. I'll watch."

Oh, how much certainty and confidence there was in that "I'll watch"! The bread came out beautifully.

And I thought to myself: Who of my old friends in the village back home knows what real happiness is? Who of them has lived through such a joyous day?

Hasidah had magic in her fingers. Whatever she did came out right. By the time the men returned from the field everything was ready. They asked her anxiously how she felt: there was an atmosphere of solicitude and respect around her. The next morning Aaron fell sick, and there was no one to follow the plough with the seed. Abraham suggested that I be taken along. There was much laughter—and yet in the end they had to take me because there was no one else. And so I was to go out on the fields! I had no idea of what I would have to do—but I was happy. The boys made room for me at the table, and called out: "Sit next to me, *fellah.* . ." All day long I went after the plough, and dropped the seed. I did not get tired. Around me I heard voices: "Good work." In the evening I returned on horseback, my hair falling loose over my shoulder. I did not care; I felt well, I was happy. On the porch stood the nurse, together with Hasidah. She had come to attend to Aaron. I rode up to the pair of them and sprang off my horse. I wanted to run to Hasidah, take her aside, pour out all my joy; but her cool look froze the words on my lips. The nurse exclaimed:

"What youth! What health!"

Hasidah answered: "Just a girl—like all the others. Out there, in the fields, among the boys, she becomes another person. And all the kitchen work falls on me again."

I hear her, and I understand her only too well. And I ask myself what this attitude of hers means. What am I to deduce from it? Have I any right to stay on here? She calls me "Little girl"—but I want to be a worker. I must make up my mind what to do.

That evening I did not go in to dinner. And when they asked "Where's the *fellah?*" they were told "in bed." "No wonder," they said, "after that long day in the sun." I did not close my eyes that night, and I could not decide on a course of action. It was impossible to return to Jaffa, to have them say: "Our little worker is back so soon?" And I could not stay on. I had heard enough to make me feel that I was not wanted.

VIII

EARLY the next morning, the train brought a welcome visitor, Kotick, the Secretary. They clustered round him in the dining-room, asking for the news, but the first thing he said was: "Where's that little comrade that just came here? I have a letter for her from her brother Ezra."

I took the letter, and felt myself turning pale. "If you want," Kotick said, "you can send an answer through me. I'm leaving for Jerusalem tomorrow."

Ezra wrote that he had been persuaded to go to Jerusalem, and he was not sorry at all. Things were going well with him and he had a nice room. If I wanted, I could come to him for a little time; Kotick, who was a good friend of his, would advance me the money for the fare. The letter was like the voice of a deliverer! I could leave the *kvutzah* without going back to Jaffa! I was saved!

When breakfast was over, I went up to Kotick, and in a low, timid voice told him that Ezra had asked me to come to him, and that he, Kotick, might lend me the money.

"Why, certainly," he said, with a charming smile.

Then I added: "And, if you won't find it a burden, I'd like to travel together with you."

"Of course," he said, eagerly. "Ezra's little sister. . ."

The comrades looked at me in amazement. They began to ask me: "Are you really leaving? Why has your brother sent for you? When are you coming back?" I did not answer. Only Hasidah seemed to be satisfied.

"Well, what did I tell you? A child. Your *fellah*. She's been here a few days and she's off to Jerusalem." And suddenly she became very serious. "Pity she went into the fields yesterday. My room hasn't been cleaned once since I was sick."

"There's still time," I said. "Kotick isn't going till twelve o'clock tomorrow. And if there's no other work for me, I'll start on your room at once."

Hasidah's face lit up. "Will you really? Let's carry the things out, and I'll prepare whitewash for you. And if you'll whitewash the room for me, I'll have something to remember you by."

"What do you mean, 'remember her by'?" Abraham put in. "How long do you think she's going to stay in Jerusalem?"

But no one answered him, and Abraham turned away depressed. I threw myself into the work, and in it almost forgot my hurt and my anger. I did my best to make a straight line of whitewash, to keep it from sprinkling the windows and running down on the floor. When the whitewashing was done I washed all the floors, and in the evening I helped Hasidah carry the things back into her room. Hasidah looked thoughtful. "How clean it is!" Then after a pause, she added: "Suppose you did come back, after all. It wasn't so bad here, was it?"

When the comrades returned, they talked in low tones about me. I learned afterwards that they felt guilty; they had not treated me as they should have done. They wanted to persuade me to stay. Or perhaps Hasidah could persuade me to come back after a short stay in Jerusalem.

And sure enough, in the morning, Hasidah said to me:
"I forgot to ask you when you're coming back. We were
so busy all yesterday that we hadn't time to talk it over."

"I'm not coming back," I said, shortly.

"But why? Do you find the work too hard? Never mind
that. Come back. You're too young, I know, but I'll teach
you everything, and you'll like it here. And listen, Amunah, I've got a half-pound saved up. I've been thinking a
long time of buying myself a pretty dress, and now you're
going to Jerusalem, perhaps you'll buy the material for
me. You're a good judge. I'll leave it to you."

She went over to her basket and began to rummage in it.
From underneath the books she dragged out a brown
dress, a heritage of her half-forgotten student days in
Russia. But to her horror she found that the mice had
eaten away the pocket and the half pound with it. But I
had no sympathy for her at that moment: for this was
my revenge. She had kept money of her own in the
kvutzah! How was such a thing possible?

IX

KOTICK knocked at my door. "Little girl, it's time to
start out. We can't have the wagon today, it's needed
for the sowing. We'll have to make the station on foot.
Get ready."

All the way to Jerusalem Kotick did his best to keep me
cheerful. He did not care that I could not speak Hebrew.
He spoke Yiddish and Russian to me. But I hardly answered a word. I was thinking how I would face my
brother Ezra, and what I would say to *him*.

We knocked a long time at my brother's door, and finally
he came out. "I didn't hear you—I was writing letters.
Oh, Amunah, so you came! You're not sick, are you? I
suppose you came just to see Jerusalem."

I was silent. I felt the tears gathering in my eyes, but

my brother's "nice" room was so small that I could not turn
away from him.

That day we hardly spoke. The next morning, when
Ezra had gone out, I sat down at the table to write. I did
not notice the passing of the time, and it seemed I had
scarcely begun before Ezra was back for the noon-day
meal.

"Are you writing mother?" he asked.

"No, I'm writing you," I answered. "Every time I want
to tell you what happened, I feel like crying. So I'll tell
it to you on paper instead." And I handed him what I
had written.

He looked through it earnestly, and then he said: "Promise me you won't write any more. Writing makes people
old; it throws a shadow over their lives. And you're only
a little girl. Don't go in for such things. It's better for you
to learn how to bake bread and milk cows. That's a lot
more important in Palestine."

x

A week passed, and there was very little conversation
between us. All day Ezra was at work, and I passed most
of the time reading the few books he had obtained for
me.

Then one evening we sat down to talk it out. And the
first question he asked me was whether I had liked the
comrades in the *kvutzah*.

"No," I said. "The only one I liked was Abraham. He's
a nice boy. He helped me with everything."

"Oh, Abraham is the nice boy, is he? You're still very
simple, little sister. You happen to be young, and not
downright ugly, and that's why he enjoyed helping you."

"You've such a queer way of talking to me," I said,
impatiently. "You remind me of an old schoolteacher
who's afraid to say something nice in case it spoils you."

"What did I say now?"

" 'Not downright ugly'."

"Oh, all right. Do you want me to say you're beautiful? Your eyes look quite clever—but you're not too clever at that."

We both burst out laughing.

One evening we came back from a lecture. My brother put his hands on my shoulders and said:

"Confess, Amunah, what's in your mind. Aren't you thinking how you'd like to stand on the platform and deliver a lecture like that?"

"You're a million miles out," I said. "I was thinking how I'd like to be able to bake bread and milk cows. That's the only thing I care about—and you've got to help me again. I can't stay here idle any longer. You told me that you've got a friend on the training farm, and that if you wrote him he'd manage to get me in. Write to him now."

My brother shrugged his shoulders. "I'll write," he said. "But don't walk around that way, and don't be on pins and needles till you get your answer. This time I won't send you out alone."

It was Kotick himself who came with the answer. He walked in early one morning, with a letter. "You don't have to read it," he said, laughing. "I know what's in it. You're going to the village to milk cows! I was present at the meeting where it was decided to take you on. And I'm going to accompany you out there, too, because I'm going back in a couple of days. Only this time you've got to promise to be a little more cheerful."

My last morning in Jerusalem I had given my brother the manuscript that I had written during my stay with him. He had read it through with deep interest, and now, when I was getting ready to leave, he said: "I honestly don't know how to talk with you. If I talk to you as to a child, you'll be offended. And if I treat you like a grown-up, you won't understand me." He tapped the manuscript. "But I'll treat you like a grown-up. Your writing lacks

style and language. It's not intelligible. And yet there's
something in it. If you didn't want to be a worker, it
might be worth spending time on it. But as it is—I can't
see it."

"If you treat me like a grown-up," I said, "I'll answer
you like one. You're deliberately belittling my writing.
Show me one sentence that isn't intelligible."

My brother looked through the manuscript again.
"Here: 'A girl can marry and be happy even at seventeen,
as my friend has done; but only a grown-up person can be
happy in a *kvutzah*.' "

"You didn't understand that?" I asked. I snatched the
manuscript from his hand and tore it into scraps. My
brother stared at me.

"What did you do that for?"

"I only wanted to show you that my writing means
nothing to me. And you may be sure that I shan't lose
a single hour of work for the sake of it. But it wasn't
necessary for you to belittle it."

Kotick came in hastily without knocking.

"Quick now," he said. "We haven't a minute to lose if
we want to make the train."

"I'm ready," I said. "Goodbye, brother."

"Goodbye, sister." And holding my hand, he added:
"And so the cows are going to win out?"

"That's my big hope," I answered.

Ain Charod   B. B.

PART II
WITH THE GROUP

II

WITH THE GROUP

THE KVUTZAH OF TWENTY

IT WAS a fearful and difficult time—the third year of
the World War. The threat of utter ruin hung over the
Jewish settlement in Palestine. The comrades whom we
could not employ were taken up by the government for
public works, and they labored like slaves for a meagre
sustenance. But while they at least had enough, or nearly
enough, to keep body and soul together, the women had
nothing at all. Their condition was one of destitution
and desperation. They used to wander from one workers'
kitchen to another, from colony to colony, from *kvutzah*
to *kvutzah,* seeking work. But there was no work; and
they would not eat the bread of charity. And so they
covered the country from end to end, hungry and un-
wanted.

And at last the first victim fell. The young Miriam
Greenblatt, a quiet, deeply thoughtful girl, took her own
life. A shudder ran through the Jewish settlement. The
incident was seen as a warning. The long negotiations
which had been conducted with various groups and institutions had brought no real results; now it was realised
something had to be done at once.

Joseph Busel came forward with a proposition. (Busel
was one of the founders of the colony Deganiah, a pro-
tagonist of the collectivist idea for the workers of Palestine.
He was drowned in the Sea of Galilee in 1919.) The un-

employed women workers of Galilee were to organise
themselves into a *kvutzah*. The *kvutzah* of Kinereth and
the farm school of Hannah Meisel promised the new group
a patch of twenty dunams (five acres) for a vegetable
garden. But the chief income would come from outside
work. Some of the women would do the cooking for the
men who were draining the Kinereth swamps. Others, we
hoped, would find seasonal employment in the neighboring *kvutzoth* of Kinereth and Deganiah. There were some
women who could sew, and they too hoped to find some
sort of employment at their trade. At the instance of
Busel, the Zionist bureau in Jaffa advanced to the "unemployed" *kvutzah* sixty pounds for tools and other initial
expenses.

We jumped at this plan. Hannah Meisel promised to
act as our advisory expert. She put only one condition:
she wanted the Women Workers' Council of Galilee to
appoint two skilled and experienced comrades to take
charge of the social life and the work of the new *kvutzah*.
But skilled and experienced comrades were exactly what
we lacked. After an inner struggle with myself, and
against my inclination, I offered myself. I knew what a
responsibility I was taking on myself, but the situation was
desperate and there was no other way out.

The majority of these unemployed women were strangers
to each other; and they became acquainted only as members of the *kvutzah*. There was a wide range of ages, of
outlook and of development, a motley of human material
bound together for the time by the common misfortune of
unemployment. At our first meeting we discussed the
difficult task and the heavy responsibility which we had
assumed. In my own speech I tried to express the genuine
fear which I felt. I was not sure that we had in our midst
the forces which would enable us to carry out our plans,
and establish the *kvutzah* on a permanent foundation. But
the meeting was enthusiastic, and a spirit of helpfulness
showed itself. We chose there and then the council of

the *kvutzah,* consisting of three: Shoshana Bogen, Hannah Katzenelson and myself.

The first question was of quarters. Where were we to live? Days passed in fruitless search. The workers did not use tents at that time; these came in only after the war, with the third tide of immigration. And new houses were not being built, for the price of materials was prohibitive.

At last in the Kinereth *kvutzah* we secured a room adjoining the stables. The windows looked out toward the threshing floor and the highway, and so we got our fill of dust and stable smells. Another, smaller, room was lower down in the colony, on the shore of the Sea of Galilee. We divided the larger room with a curtain. In one half we worked and ate; here, too, we kept the big box of wheat which we obtained from the *Mashbir* cooperative. On the other side of the curtain were fourteen very original "beds." A bed consisted of three empty gasolene cans covered with boards and straw matting. The beds stood so close to each other that in the night we would dig elbows into each other. Near the large room there was a tiny cubicle, without flooring and unwhitewashed. We cleaned this out, installed a stove—and we had a kitchen.

From the day when we began to work our garden, the *kvutzah* considered itself as officially established. Every evening the Council of Three apportioned the work for the next day, made up the accounts, and gave directives generally.

The work which some of the women had to do was heavy and unpleasant. Other luckier ones were assigned lighter tasks. But the luckiest were those who were privileged to work in our own garden. However, the garden was small, and not more than a couple of women could be employed here at one time.

Let me say that from the outset, in spite of the fact the women had not known each other when they came together, a strong feeling of common responsibility devel-

oped at once. They obeyed the orders of the council even
when they did not agree with them, and even when they
had protested against them at the meetings of the *kvutzah*.
The social discipline which was displayed was not the
result of force; it sprang spontaneously from a healthy
sense of responsibility.

It was only after the war that the special type of commune arose which takes in people who do not know each
other. Before that the *kvutzoth* consisted always of friends,
and new comrades were admitted only after long counsel.
In its time, therefore, our *kvutzah* was something of a
phenomenon; and, curiously enough, it made a name for
itself by reason of the spirit of comradeliness which reigned
in it.

We were poorly fed, for we budgeted our meals, and
would under no circumstances go beyond our resources.
We were determined not to get into debt. But when the
Kinereth summer was added to the burden of our work
and undernourishment, we began to go down with malaria.
The strong and healthy took on double burdens; the weak
did what they could. Most of the time they were unfit
even for light tasks. They had to lie around hoping that
the slender help given them by the *Kupat Cholim*, the
Workers' Sick Fund, would cure them.

Winter evenings we ate by the light of a tiny wick
dipped in oil; after which we would keep our only kerosene
lamp burning for two hours while we read and prepared
our lectures. There were three groups living in that yard,
the Kinereth *kvutzah*, Hannah Meisel's training farm, and
we. During the week there were scientific courses and
language lessons. Saturday we studied the Bible. This
yard was the focus of our common spiritual life. We got
together a fine choir, and besides the singing there were
interesting, comradely talks round the table of the Kinereth
kvutzah. Our group of women participated in everything.
In spite of the poverty and privation, this happy little room
became a centre of attraction; but those who were drawn

to us most, and toward whom we reciprocated the feeling, were the swamp workers. There was a special bond between us. They, like us, had been among the unemployed yesterday. And now they were proud of our successful *kvutzah.*

Now there was no shortage of work, for we put our hands to whatever turned up. Our one worry was to pay back as quickly as possible the loan from the Zionist Organisation. Our garden flourished, and there were customers for its produce. And if something was left, we used to load it onto donkeys and take it up the hills to Puriah, where we sold it to some American families and to government officials, or perhaps to the farm-workers themselves. Then we would come back singing to our happy "home" next door to the stable. Our patch of soil was so fruitful that we paid off almost the entire debt, and would have paid all of it if not for the merciless *Osher* (tithe) which was exacted by the Government.

There were no contractual obligations in our *kvutzah.* If a woman found work elsewhere she was free to go, and we would find someone to replace her. A year passed in this way. By that time, however, our numbers had dwindled to six, for most of the workers had found permanent positions. With my five companions I went over to Merchaviah, and there we founded a new *kvutzah* of women workers, not of the unemployed.

Deganiah Aleph   JAEL GORDON.

ON THE RUN

Two o'clock they made the rounds, and woke all of us. The comrades of the *kvutzah* Achvah were to gather for a meeting in the workers' club. A host of refugees had just arrived in Petach Tikvah, and something had to be done. Hassan Bek, the Turkish official, had driven them out of Jaffa and Tel Aviv in order to keep Jews away from the front. (Passover, 1917.)

There were in hiding among us comrades from every corner of the country. They were hiding from the agents of the Turkish government, from the periodic searches and seizures. In our house—as in every other—there was not a corner which was not occupied; and I was tired out by the day's heavy work, and by the unceasing tumult around me. Moreover, I was almost broken by the miseries which these expulsions brought in their wake. Yet, when I was called at two in the morning to this meeting, I got up. A great many others had come, too. Joseph Chaim Brenner* was among them.

And the subject of the talk was—our responsibility toward the homeless. We had an obligation toward them, as toward the whole Palestinian settlement. We could not be content with giving them shelter merely as long as they stayed with us in Tel Aviv. We had to do more. We had to look after them until they had found some sort of permanent refuge.

The brutality of the Government grew from day to day, and conditions naturally grew worse. The arrests increased, and among the chief sufferers were the leaders

*One of the most gifted Hebrew writers. Killed by Arabs in the riots of 1921.

of the Poale Zion (the Zionist Socialist Party) and the comrades of *Ha-Shomer,* the Guards organisation. Then the Government issued a last warning, in which it demanded, under threat of the severest repressive measures, that all men of military age should report to headquarters. Among the workers in Petach Tikvah there were some of Austrian citizenship. In order to make up the tally of the number of men who were expected to report, they decided to give themselves up. They believed that, being the nationals of an allied power, they would be released at once. Three of them died in the Damascus prison. After the war, when a new workers' settlement was formed in Petach Tikvah, we named it Givath Shloshah, "The Hill of the Three," a memorial to the three Galician comrades who had given their lives for us.

Refugees came daily into Petach Tikvah. The streets were filled with them; and every day an old Sephardic Jew wandered among them, crying in a hoarse, melancholy voice: "God has commanded that you obey the laws of the state. In the next twenty-four hours you must all go to Galilee, and evil will befall him who does not go." (This old man was engaged for this purpose by the Turkish government; he was one of the "town-criers" who used to acquaint towns and villages with new decrees.)

At the night meeting which we held in the workers' club, I decided to go with a group of emigrants to Galilee; I wanted to work among their younger daughters, who were surrounded by particularly great dangers.

I was also charged, at that time, with difficult and responsible tasks for the Poale Zion Party. Often, without realising how dangerous it was, I would act as liaison between the scattered points, carrying the word from comrade to comrade. But however necessary my work in Judaea was, I thought that Galilee took precedence over it.

The streams of immigrants turned toward the town of Tiberias, and few of them were to be found in the Galilee

colonies. In Tiberias the hunger grew from day to day.
With hunger came infectious diseases, and families began
to dwindle. A relief committee was formed, at the head
of which was M. Dizengoff, later mayor of Tel Aviv. Dizengoff went up to Damascus, to maintain communications
between the Palestinian settlement and world Jewry. To
Damascus came the contributions of world Jewry. Joseph
Busel was still alive; he was the workers' representative
on the committee, and on him fell the difficult responsibility
of settling the immigrants in some new location.

All the refugees suffered, but the girls suffered most.
They were hungry and idle, and life lost all its savor for
them. Tiberias was filled with soldiers, mostly Germans
who were then the masters in Palestine. Money and provisions were plentiful among them, and a fearful wave
of prostitution spread through the starving town. Fearful
scenes took place, often among the most pious families;
and the greatest sufferers from the calamity were the
Sephardic Jews.

When I arrived in Tiberias, and saw the situation for
myself, I decided that the first thing to be done was to
create a women workers' *kvutzah* for the young immigrants. I worked out the details, prepared a budget, and
brought the plan to Joseph and Hiutah Busel. Both of
them were ready to help; they were joined by two other
skilled women comrades, Rachel Rosenfeld and Nehamah
Sitzer. Busel obtained for us a loan of a hundred francs
with which to lease the garden which we were to work.
No sooner was the information out, than dozens of young
girls, the daughters of immigrant families, applied. But
the number of free places was limited, and the list was at
once filled.

Busel persuaded the relief committee to make special
arrangements for the *kvutzah*. Instead of the *rutel* (six
and a half pounds) of flour a week which was distributed
to every person in the town, the *kvutzah* obtained a loan
for three months' provisions. The loan was to be paid back

as soon as the vegetable garden began to produce an income.

And now we were ready to dig. But where were we to get seed?

One day, when the heavens were pouring themselves out in rain, I went out of Tiberias to Kinereth. It was known in Galilee that I had been one of the lucky ones who had remained "in England" (this was the current name for Judæa, which fell into English hands in the fall of 1917, while Galilee remained Turkish until the end of 1918). Comrades were amazed at me. Why had I left the happy soil of Judaea and thrown myself into the hunger and suffering of Galilee?

In Kinereth I went straight to Meyer Rutberg, one of the founders of the new consumers' coperative of the Labor Federation—*Ha-Mashbir*. I asked him to make a loan to the three members of the *Histadruth* (Federation) who were working with the immigrant girls. The loan was to consist of seed for the garden, and grain for bread. The military forces in the country needed great quantities of vegetables. The German mark was at that time secure; and as soon as the garden produced we would pay back the loan in full.

I returned to Tiberias with seed and grain, and we plunged heartily into the work. We planted cabbages, onions, potatoes and cucumbers. Everything took well, everything shot up.

Within a short time our little *kvutzah* had become the cultural focus of Tiberias. Teachers among the immigrants lectured in our *kvutzah,* and the Jews of Tiberias looked with respect on our girls, as they went through the streets early in the morning and late in the evening with their spades on their shoulders.

The two loans, from the committee and from *Ha-Mashbir* were not enough to see us through. And just when supplies gave out, the most exacting work began—the digging. Starvation stared us in the face. Among the comrades there were some who even had to share their daily ration with their families. More than once I saw one of the girls leave the line, tear up some grass from the field, and try to still the pangs of hunger. There were times when we thought it impossible to go on.

The vegetables began to ripen, and it was necessary to set a watch in the night against thieves. We could not pay a watchman, and therefore we became guards, too. I was the first to go on sentry duty.

It was a Saturday night. I had made the round of the garden once, and was just returning to my post when I stumbled against something that loomed black in the darkness. An Arab wrapped in a black *abaya* got up out of the onion patch. I uttered such a wild scream that I almost frightened the life out of myself.

The garden lay outside the town. No one heard me, and no one came to help me. I remained in the place until morning, and next day we decided to set two guards. We trembled most of all for our onions, because they had come up beautifully. When we finally began to take in some money for our produce, life in the *kvutzah* became more tolerable. And when the potatoes ripened, and they had to be guarded in turn, we were able to engage a watchman. But in a few days we had to dismiss him, because apparently the thieves and he ignored each other! We returned to guard duty ourselves.

I remember particularly a certain Friday night. I had gone out with two comrades on the watch. We spread ourselves a mat in the middle of the garden, and sat there talking quietly. From time to time we got up and made the rounds. The first half of the night passed peacefully. In the second half we were suddenly aware of the noise of a multitude approaching: hordes of Turkish soldiers were passing along the road by the garden.

It was shortly before Passover. Apparently preparations were being made in the night for a new offensive. All of us were seized with the same thought: the hungry Turkish soldiers might break into the garden in search of food and find—us! I signalled to the other two women to remain absolutely silent. I tried to appear calm, but I was trembling from head to foot. At every instant I expected to hear the closer tread of approaching feet. Only with the dawn, when the Arab guards in the neighboring gardens left their posts, we got up from our places and went home, exhausted and broken.

The happy time arrived at last. Big military trucks came rolling toward our garden. The yield was a rich one, the prices were steady, and we made money. Then we decided to begin paying back the loans to the committee and *Ha-Mashbir*.

That first day was a day of triumph and victory. All of us gathered in the little room, and with much ceremony we deposited the first payment in the safe—which consisted of an old tea can. We even drew lots to fix on the lucky person who would have the privilege of taking the first payment to the committee. Hasidah was the one to draw the winning number. She put on holiday dress and danced rather than walked into town.

We paid all our debts and still had something left. Every comrade in the *kvutzah* got a bonus—a franc for every working day. And even to the watchmen who had worked a few nights for us we sent their extra share.

Chavurath ha-Zaphon, Tel Aviv   HANNAH CHISICK.

IN THE DAYS OF HASSAN BEK*

IT WAS in Kinereth in the month of Cheshvan (October) 1917. The days were still hot, and the nights magically clear. Every day new stories reached us of the sufferings of the Jews in Judæa, Jerusalem and Samaria at the hands of the Turks. A systematic search for military evaders was being conducted. Our boys were taken away to forced labor with the Turkish military; most of them were in the transport, driving heavy loads from Beersheba in the south to Metulah in the north. We heard that the Turks were making special efforts to locate arms. They had already searched Merchaviah and Tel Adas. In particular they were looking for the comrades of *Ha-Shomer*, the Jewish guard organisation. At that time I knew nothing about the espionage story, or about the English arms in our possession.

In the summer nights there would be raids of bandits. We, the girls, used to sleep on the roof, and we were frequently awakened by the shooting. Sometimes the boys would go out, and be absent for hours in the hills, driving off the raiders.

The Turks came to us in Kinereth too. "The Commission," as we called it, came early one morning. I remember how the news reached me. I was told that the men had been called out for an examination—every male in the colony, including the old and sick. They had been taken away, but we believed that they would soon return. But

---

*Chassan Bek, an Arab of Aleppo, military doctor with the Turks, who headed the Commission investigating espionage among the Jews for the British forces. The investigations were carried out with particular ruthlessness in Zichron Jacob, Tel Adas and Kinereth. His name struck terror into everybody.

hours passed, and there was no sign of them. Reports began to spread that they had been taken onto the bridge across the Jordan, and were being beaten unmercifully. The girls who were bringing them food were caught, and were being whipped. I went down to the bridge, and among the prisoners huddled together there, I saw also Joseph Baratz—the only man who had been taken from the colony of Deganiah.

As often as I tried to pass -over to the prisoners, the guards approached me offensively. I had to exert all my will-power in order not to spit in their faces; but I knew that in their hands lay the fate of our men. Within a few days we had managed to accustom ourselves to the new, strange conditions. The girls in the colony took over all the work, and did double duty in the barns and the fields. They supplied the soldiers who came for food and fodder. One moment I remember, when I was sweeping the stables. M. was outside—he had not been arrested—and he was watering the animals. He strolled casually up to the window and winked at me: there was so much courage and hope and endurance in that wink of his that I felt myself strengthened . . .

The Turkish officers beat our men and threatened that, if they did not reveal where the weapons were, they would plough up all our fields. Actually they did nothing. They did not even set up a guard in the yard of the *kvutzah*.

The boys had slipped the information to me where the weapons were concealed, and Aaron Sher (who was killed afterwards in Tel Hai) explained to me the difference between English and Turkish guns. I understood that the first things to be gotten rid of were the English guns, though I didn't quite see why they were more dangerous than the Turkish. I looked through the stable loft and found the boxes of English guns under a huge mound of hay; with them were several packages of English guns and cartridges. In the night we determined to move the supplies from this dangerous place. We lowered the packages of ammunition into the toilet cans; we were sure that no one would look there. While we worked we heard suddenly the creaking of wheels outside—and we stood still, as if paralysed. The creaking passed and we went on with our work. We decided to get the guns down to the Sea of Galilee, and throw them in. We took them out, and by moonlight stole down the water's edge, the guns slung on our shoulders. There we skirted the water till we found a deep place, and let the guns down. Several times we made the journey back and forth. One of the women on this job was the mother of a small child. Until this day I shudder, and wonder at our marvelous luck in not being caught. But there was not a soul to be seen; it was as if the earth had swallowed the Turkish soldiers. When the task was done there was a sort of freshness in the air around, and in our hearts too. The next morning the soldiers turned up to arrest all of us. Sher pretended to be sick. When he tried to get out of his bed he acted so realistically that I was terrified. But soon I understood that he really wanted someone to bring him a glass of water. When I gave it to him he whispered that this night we would have to place three guns and packages of cartridges under the date tree at the foot of Kerok hill. I did not know the meaning of this, but I felt that it had to be done. It was with the utmost difficulty that I persuaded two women to help me. I told them, as I remember, that on this depended our lives and the lives of our comrades. I spoke so earnestly, so wildly, that they agreed—it was almost as if I had hypnotised them. And that night we put on black shawls and hid the guns under them. We had agreed that we were "going out to find a black cow that had got lost." And instead of walking stealthily, we went out into the darkness calling "Hey, Blackie, Blackie, where are you?" In this way we managed to place the guns and cartridges in the appointed place. When I got back I collapsed on my bed, seized with a horrible cramp; nothing was wrong with me—only my nerves had given way.

During the days that followed I could not eat. I would go up to the table and put a black olive in my mouth, but it would not go down. The girls worked like draft animals; all the burden of the *kvutzah* had fallen on them. But I could do nothing. Nor did they ask me to do my share. I was reserved for something else: I received secret instructions and obeyed them. I asked no questions. I did what I was told to do.

I learned before long the purpose for which the three guns had been hidden under the date tree. Sher, A. Z., and F. pretended to give way under the bastinado and confessed that they were the three shepherds of Kinereth, and they had hidden their weapons under the tree. They believed that in this way they would relieve the whole colony. And I think I saw them in the night being led away by a convoy, their heads down, the guns carried by soldiers.

In a few days ben-Zion was set free, and the first ray of hope shone on us. The same night I, together with ben-Zion and young Michael (a fine, lovable boy who was wounded later in Upper Galilee and died in horrible anguish in the hospital of Tiberias) carried out of the buildings the rest of the guns. We hid them in the gulch which cuts across our fields. That night we were crazy with joy, like people who had escaped from death and were now going to rescue their comrades.

A few days later the other boys were transferred to the prison in Tiberias. I followed, took a room in a hotel near by and brought them food every day. I trembled that the food might not reach them, that some of them might be transferred where I could not look after them or that something worse might happen—hanging was not impossible. In particular we were uncertain about the lives of the three, Sher, A. Z., and F. And there was no news of them. It only seemed to me that sometimes, when I went to the prison, I would catch sight of a familiar face.

I remember trying to chum up with the wives of some of the arrested planter colonists. These women spoke French, and might be able to find out something. But they shied away from me. Those days brought friends closer together than ever before, but they also widened the gulf between strangers.

One evening, when I returned to my hotel, afraid as always of bed news, I was told that Sher and A. Z. had called during the day, on their way back to Kinereth! They were at home now, and our rejoicing was all the deeper because secretly we had scarcely dared to hope that we would ever see them again. The next day I returned once more to Tiberias. There I learned that the other prisoners had been sent on to Nazareth, and there was no more reason for me to stay on.

Herzliah   FRIDA.

TWENTY-FOUR HOURS

AFTER a day's work in the kitchen, hungry and exhausted, I lay down to sleep. My "home" was a little hut on the shore of Galilee; it had three rooms—a kitchen, a living room, and a cubicle which was store-room and pantry.

I had taken up half the store-room for my "bed"—the usual bed of those days, planks on empty gasolene cans. But for a long time I could not sleep. The mice would not let me. They squeaked and fought around me, jumping in and out of the empty pea and bean cans.

And lying there, I ask myself: What will happen to-morrow? There's not enough in the house to feed a puppy. If we look long enough we may scrape up a glassful of peas, but suppose I have got soup enough for twenty men—what about the next meal? These men come home from the fields hungry. And what shall I give them with the tea? It's so long since we've seen sugar we've forgotten what it looks like. The raisin supply is a memory. Food is scarce and money even scarcer—in fact, there is none . . . It's no good thinking; better try to sleep. I draw the sheet over my head, scared that the mice will start playing with my two long braids.

Suddenly, a knock at the window. I answer out of my sleep: "Who's there?"

"It's me."

I recognise the voice of one of the comrades. "What is it?" I ask.

"Open the window, and take this."

I look up at the window, and make out a rifle, a belt and a bag of loose cartridges.

"What shall I do with it?"

"Hide it in a safe place."

I go to the window and take gun, belt and cartridges. He adds: "We don't know what'll happen tomorrow. We just had a meeting. The decisions are secret."

"All right," I say. "You don't have to tell. Shalom!"

I close the window and lie down again. Secret decisions . . . dangers . . . no one must know. . . . My thoughts will not rest. Of late the men comrades have been behaving queerly at their work; things are not going smoothly. I know nothing, understand nothing. A secret decision is a secret decision. Again I cover myself. There's a heavy day ahead of me, I must rest. I must sleep. I must sleep. And at last I fall into a doze.

Again a knock at the window. "Nechamah, are you still sleeping? Nechamah!"

I start up. "Get up, Nechamah. The shepherds have been arrested." And she names my two friends. "The colonists have been arrested, too. No one's safe."

I go to the window again. Dawn has come. The sun is just lying level on the Sea of Galilee. The picture rises again before me—but I understand nothing; the words of the Sephardic girl convey nothing.

She goes on: "Everyone's been arrested. Look! police everywhere." I look out. Near my door stands a policeman, and the meaning of it all becomes clear to me. I begin to storm.

"Listen," I said to the girl, "I can't speak Arabic. Tell him girls are sleeping in here. Tell him to get out."

She tells him, and he does take himself off, but not far. He stops at a little distance from the house.

I work hastily, and pack into the bed everything that my comrade had handed over to me. Then I cover it all up, so that it looks as though someone were sleeping there. Then I slip out to see what has happened.

I go down to the colony. The girls are going about their work, and they will not speak. In the *kvutzah* yard, again, only girls. The men have been taken away. I meet Zipporah,

a relative of comrade A. Passing by, she tells me in stacca-
to whispers: "Listen! careful—the police are watching! A.'s
house is just full of that stuff. We've got to get it out of
the way before the search starts. Can you do it?"

That was all I needed. We passed each other, and understood without further parley that we were to meet as
soon as possible in A.'s house.

I go down the slope. The house is surrounded by police.
I ignore them and pass right into the house. A.'s parents
are there, in a panic. I soothe them. They themselves do
not know what dangerous stuff there is in the house, but
they feel blindly that some disaster is impending. In a few
minutes Zipporah turned up; and we began to feel better.

As the police kept away, we set to work at once. We
placed the guns in baskets, and heaped loaves of bread and
tomatoes on top. When I was through I told Zipporah that
I was going out to work in Hannah Meisel's garden, and
I went out with a basket.

Hannah Meisel's garden was surrounded by a barbed
wire fence and with yellow acacia, so closely grown that
it was impossible to take a short cut through. When I got
round to the gate I saw that all the girls were outside—a
white flood poured over the green, square-cut patches.

And here too, all round the field, a chain of policemen.
"Girls, girls!" I shout. "Eats!"

In an instant the girls had surrounded me and began to
empty the basket. Meanwhile I pretended to do some work
with the spade, and a few minutes later I returned to A.'s
house. In this way I smuggled through basket after basket.
And just when I left with the last basket, I heard carriage
bells on the road. "The Commission" had arrived to look
for weapons, and the first point they made for was A.'s
house.

All's well. The house has been cleared—but here I am
with the last basket in my hand. No sense in running—
they'd stop me at once. I walk slowly, the spade over my
shoulder, the basket in my hand. I sing loudly and cheer-

fully: *"Uru Achim, al tanumu, l'avodatchem uru, kumu,"* and singing I pass through the field, into the farm. There everything has been looked after.

Enough for one day.

And then, like a flame leaping up in me, I remember the "goods" I had left lying around in my room. It is noon. I have had neither bite nor sup, and I am exhausted. "The Commission" is in A.'s house, two doors away from my room.

I turn back, and make for my room. Every second counts now. The police are masters everywhere. But they won't get a word out of us girls. They surround us on every side, but we'll see who's quicker-witted. Too late to save the men—they're arrested. But we'll stand by this place.

I pass through a police cordon. I hear them say: *"Hadi shatre! cul yum bihstril* (A real gem of a girl; she's been at it since early morning)." So I am not suspected yet. I take out bread and tomatoes to eat—and I have my plan! I'll pretend to get the oven ready, and meanwhile I can smuggle the gun and the other stuff out. And when "the Commission" turns its back, I can really shove them into the stove.

I put the ammunition into the bucket, and went to fetch water; I put three cartridges into the Browning and slipped it on. I had made up my mind: one cartridge was for the man who tried to stop me, two were for myself.

"The Commission" had left A.'s house and paid no attention to me. It returned to Tiberias, leaving word that this same night the infamous Hassan Bek in person would visit our colony, that multiple murderer who would take things out of the hands of the police, and lash and torture his victims himself.

Now I have a little respite. I sit half-dead on the doorstep of my house. Everything has been done. But then I remember—A. must be told that his house has been cleaned out. I go over to the colony; all the prisoners are jammed into one small room.

I knock at the window and ask for comrade A. He makes his way through to me.

"Shalom!"

"Shalom!" I answer. Then quickly: "The house is cleared. The guests found nothing." I raise my voice and say in Arabic: "And what shall I do now, Sir?"

"We're terribly thirsty in here," he said. "Bring us a jug of water—but a large one."

"I understand, Sir," I answer. I went into the house of a colonist, asked for a big jug, filled it with water, took a glass, and returned to the prison. The guards would not let me go inside, but they let me pass the jug and glass through the window. In two minutes A. passed the jug back. It was considerably heavier than before. I went into the fields and emptied it.

After a time I returned to the prisoners for news. A. appeared at the window, white as chalk. He said: "P. got the bastinado. It's more than an hour since they tortured him, and he can't utter a word yet. It's better to be killed. I'm afraid they're going to start on you women now. Be strong, and show what you can do."

The men had determined among themselves that if they heard the scream of a girl they would burst the room open and rush to our help, come what might. Evening came, and we sat in the *kvutzah* with ears strained. We heard them at last—Hassan Bek and his escort. He would find no weapons with us—that much was certain now. But he would not be satisfied. His murderer's blood needed a victim—the more so, in fact, because he would find nothing.

And we on our side had also made a decision. We would gather, all of us, on the second floor of Hannah Meisel's house, and defend ourselves against dishonor. I came armed; and, though this had not been agreed upon, the other girls came armed too.

Hannah's house, lifted high above the terrace of trees and flowers, looked down toward the Sea of Galilee. Downstairs, on the ground floor, was the big kitchen and dining-room. Upstairs was the dormitory and a huge verandah which was always flooded nights with moonlight or starlight. I remembered that it was on this veranda that they laid me once, when I was stricken down with malaria. Now I was here again. Three women were watching with me. We lay and listened for the sound of approaching feet. No one came.

It is night. From time to time we send someone out to inquire what has happened to the arrested men. Comrades meet—women with various instructions and messages, each one doing her work silently and efficiently. That night several of the Kinereth colonists were put to the torture. We heard from our room the screaming and shouting that came out of the prison—a ghastly noise in the wide, still night. But no weapons were given up.

Late in the night I stole out to the prison and looked in at the window. There was not room enough for the men to stretch out. They squatted on the ground, and they sang. One of their songs was in Russian.

> *The stormy days carry us, each is a wave*
> *Driving us nearer the shore of the grave . . . .*

My heart seemed to pour out of me. Darkness all around. Not one light burned in the colony. I returned to our group, and we sat and waited interminably for developments.

The torture was resumed that same night, before the prisoners were taken to Damascus for trial. Hassan Bek did not appear, but his minions did their work well. Finally one of the prisoners broke down under the torment, and involuntarily cried out that two of the girls knew where the weapons were.

In the midst of that web of police spies, our own work was conducted swiftly. Word was brought to Zipporah and myself that it was time to get out. And before dawn we stole out of Kinereth, and ran up the hills to Puriah.

Tel Aviv   NECHAMAH ZITZER.

WITH A. D. GORDON*

THEY had divided us off, that night in Kinereth, into two rooms—one was the prison room, the other was the torture chamber. From time to time they came in for the next victim, from time to time they brought in new prisoners. Seated in the prison room we could hear the blows of the bastinado on the other side of the wall, and sometimes the screaming of the tortured man. We held our breath; the fate of the colony was in the balance.

A. D. Gordon turns up among the arrested. We do not know whether he has been caught or whether he has given himself up. But we do know that soon he will be taken into the next room—it is their habit, or their plan, to choose always the oldest and the most important.

Suddenly the old man gets up from his seat and stretches out his hands as if he were about to start dancing. He thrusts everyone aside, to clear a space for himself, snaps his fingers, and breaks into impromptu singing:

> *Let my foes torment and flay me,*
> *Let them drain me, drop by drop;*
> *There's a merry song within me*
> *Pain can never stop.*

As if glued to our places we sit there, we, the young ones, listening to the singing of the "old" man. A shudder runs through all of us.

Jerusalem   H. K.

---

*A. D. Gordon, the apostle of labor in Palestine: in middle age he turned from intellectual professional pursuits to manual labor, setting a wide example. He has been called the Tolstoi of Palestine.

A WORD TO THE LEGIONARIES

An address delivered at the farewell conference of the agricultural workers' organisation and the Palestine volunteers when the latter left with the Jewish Legion, August, 1918.

THE one thing which has prevented me from adopting an attitude of respect toward the Legion has been the question of murder.

But I have answered myself: Can it be shown by anyone that Moses, or Garibaldi, men who poured out oceans of blood, were less moral than the opponents of war? It seems to me that opposition to war springs from culture and from humanity, but not specifically from morality. And now I perceive that the real sin, the real evil, lies in the alien spirit which has been introduced in our midst ever since the Legion movement began.

At the conference of the women workers one comrade said, "Our graves will be sign-posts, pointing out the road of life and work to those who will come after us." And there were women there who found it in their hearts to applaud the speaker. How deeply it hurts me that such an attitude toward death should have developed among us. Wherever people applaud the mention of death, the ugliness of life has begun.

And I ask myself: Has anyone ever had the insolence to speak the following words to a Jewish worker of Palestine: "When you are following the plough, when you are doing guard duty at night, always remember, if a man falls on you and kills you, your name will be written into the memorials of your people, and these memorials will be translated into all the languages of mankind, and they will be read in every Jewish home"? Yet why do people dare to say to the worker now: "If you fall in battle, there will be a marble memorial for you on Mount Zion, and your name will be engraved in our books forever"? And why do the Jewish workers of Palestine accept these words calmly, as if their spirit were not alien to them? Is not this a new form of assimilation? I know that in the big world, outside there, such words carry great weight; they are forever on the lips of generals, but what have they to do with us?

It seems to me that such words are fitting only for those who have protected their lives at all costs, and with every means. But we, we who have given our lives away . . . .

Such an attitude toward life befits the inhabitants of cities, who live far from nature. But how can a land-worker applaud when he sees the grasshopper coming up to destroy the wheat which he has sown? And we who have been brought up on the idea of life, how can we applaud words of death?

When have we ever arranged magnificent funerals for our dead? When Deganiah buried the slain comrade Moses Barski, it did not even call the neighbors of Kinereth to the funeral. Over the grave of Joseph Saltzman, A. D. Gordon said a simple *Kaddish* and no one else dared to speak a word.

Nor is it a Jewish custom to glorify death. The pure, true Jewish outlook, the outlook of those Jewish land-workers who wrote the Bible, is that death is a misfortune and nothing more.

It is difficult for me to speak now of Jabotinsky. He is dear to us because, like us, he has been reborn. He is near to us because he left the language and literature of strangers, learned Hebrew, and has the same feeling for poetry as we have. But he is alien to us in the matter of his outlook on work; he does not understand the affirmative values which are created by work. And it is hard for us when such as he bring this alien spirit among us. It is even hard to speak of it.

A few days ago there was a meeting in Jaffa. Jabotinsky

spoke there, and he told the audience that once, when a superior officer had insulted him unjustly, he had answered: "Yes, sir." I went away from that meeting and heard young boys repeating, with blind enthusiasm: "Yes, sir!" I felt that these strange words were bringing poison into our blood.

Was it necessary to talk like that to grown-up, developed men before they went into the Legion? Would it not have been proper to speak in an absolutely contrary spirit—to say: "You are entering the Legion to do things which outrage your conscience, which will debase your soul; you will know that this is a sin, but you must take this sin upon yourself, together with all that is good, together with all the anguish which it will bring you"?

"Yes, sir" is darkness out of which light will never be born.

And yet there are things which may fire the soul of the Jewish worker when he enters the Legion.

We are going out to conquer men in order that we may bring them into liberating work which will teach them responsibility, consciousness of duty and tolerance—work which makes them understand the meaning of reward and punishment, which replaces blind instinct with clear vision.

We are going out to create the Hebrew language, which shall take root in the hearts and mouths of our people, as it deserves to do.

We are going out to create a united Palestine.

You are going now to Galilee. You know from your studies of history that Galilee has never found its right place in the life of our people. You know that the prophets came from Judaea and Samaria, and in the days when the Jews lived in Palestine Galilee was known as "Galilee of the Gentiles"—for the Jews there were in a minority and suffered at the hands of the majority.

Even today, when we walk out the outskirts of Migdal, there rise before our eyes, out of the waters of the Sea of Galilee, the shadows of Jesus and his followers, the Jewish fisherman who carried the Evangel to the peoples of the world. But for the Jewish people Galilee has not yet said its word; only now has it begun to speak.

Kinereth! Home of the soul! How often, in uttering its name, we are tempted to say, "Kinereth the Holy."

What is it that has spread this sanctity over Kinereth? Is it the Jordan and the Sea of Galilee? Is it the grand old man, Gordon, who has lived there? Is it the Jewish girl who first began to plant and sow in its garden? Galilee has not yet spoken its word, but that word will yet be spoken.

Here in our midst a new organisation is being formed— and it came into being at the same time as the Legion. It is the *Histadruth*, the Federation of the Jewish Workers. That organisation will fight for labor, for our language and for our land—for labor which educates, for the language which unifies, and for the Galilee of the future.

R. K.

BEHIND THE FRONT

I T WAS the oppressive year of Tel Hai, when Trumpeldor
and his companions fell at their northern outpost. It was
my lot to begin my work then—not up there in Northern
Galilee, in the danger zone, but behind the front, in Deganiah.

We seem to have forgotten what the colony Deganiah,
on the Jordan, did in that year. But I will remember it as
long as I live. For with me it was the time of life when
a person must learn to suffer and sacrifice for the good of
the whole.

Deganiah was the last Jewish settlement on the eastern
frontier of the country. Close to it began the stretches of
the Bedouin country of Transjordania. And, whenever the
Bedouins took it into their minds to make a descent for
plunder, the two Deganiahs (Deganiah Aleph and Deganiah Beth) had to encounter the first attacks. Deganiah
Aleph was a fixed *kvutzah* but Deganiah Beth was still
in transition; it was a "*kvutzah* of occupation"—a group
holding on to a Jewish position, preparing it for later permanent settlement. The comrades of Deganiah Beth still
lived in rough, hastily constructed barracks which were
perfectly useless in an attack. Behind Deganiah Beth stood
Deganiah Aleph, with its two massive stone houses, and
its stables and barns of stone. Deganiah Aleph was therefore considered the extreme eastern outpost of Jewish Palestine. For months, moreover, Deganiah was the passage-
way for the comrades who came from all parts of Palestine
up to Northern Galilee to help defend Tel Hai and K'far
Gileadi.

The land was just beginning to breathe again after the

sufferings and privations of the war years. The comrades of Deganiah were anxious to put an end to all the improvisations and irregularities which had crept into their system during the uncertain time of the war, and to begin a new economic and social life. According to the plan only eleven families were to remain in Deganiah, a total of about thirty persons. And the *kvutzah* had begun to adapt itself to the new life. Then came the incidents of Tel Hai and upset everything once more.

Many of our comrades left for Galilee, and, when they came home, they used to tell us of the fearful time through which those two remote points of the north, Tel Hai and K'far Gileadi, were passing.

And meanwhile a rumor spread that the two Deganiahs were in line for a regular Bedouin assault. We went on with our work, lived in the usual routine, but we were without inner peace. Until one morning black dots began to move on the far-off horizon. These were the Bedouin horsemen; and true to our forebodings, they made first for the wooden barracks of Deganiah Beth. Trenches had been dug round these barracks, but it was thought better to withdraw the men to Deganiah Aleph. From the distance we saw our comrades setting fire to their barracks before they withdrew.

In Deganiah Aleph the safest place was the second floor of the big house. That was the centre of our system of defense. There we kept our children and the children of Deganiah Beth. In the night no one undressed. The house, the kitchen and the stables lost their ordinary character, and became strategic units. Every unit was in charge of some responsible comrade.

I and another woman comrade had to be in the second house, which contained the dining-room, the kitchen and the bakery. We also had there a small pharmacy with the most essential medicines. We set up our watch in the bakery. The most important point in our building was the kitchen. The dining-room was too exposed—it had win-

dows on three sides; and therefore the best centre of defense was the kitchen.

I do not remember how many days we passed there in
the bakery. But I do remember that the element of fear was
completely absent. Only one woman, who had come to Palestine only a short time before the events of that year,
left Deganiah. None of the other women thought of leaving
the place, or of sending away their little ones.

We lived for some time in this state of siege, and then
slowly things began to quiet down around us.

Detachments of Jewish soldiers were distributed throughout our district. We were, after all, under the protection
of England, and did not that mean security?

When the Deganiah section had quieted down, there
was still Galilee to be taken care of, and ours was a sort
of station for the men who went up there. There were times
when we had dozens of men quartered on us. We had to
look after them, and help them to continue their journey
to the posts of danger. We never knew at the beginning
of the day how many mouths we would be cooking for;
and besides the problem of food, there was always the
laundry of the strangers to be washed and mended, and
even their sick to be tended.

For not one of these transients failed to get at least
one day's meals and one night's lodgings and, if he fell
sick, the comradely care which he needed.

Nahalal   JUDITH BRONTMAN.

THE WORKERS' CLUB

MY FIRST welcome to Palestine was a long affair; it lasted
no less than three months, for that was the time that it
took me to find my first job. At last I was able to get into
the kitchen of the workers' club of Jaffa (Tel Aviv did not
exist yet) as a cook. In the yard of the club there was a sort
of ruin which could by courtesy be called a room. Because I
had children to look after, I was accorded the privilege of
making our home in that ruin.

Before coming to Palestine I had belonged to a political
party which knew of only two "races": the workers and
their oppressors. When I was in Palestine my comrades
abroad still used to send me literature to my new address—
I lived in Joseph Chaim Brenner's house. He would bring
the packages in to me without saying a word. Before long
I had accumulated quite a little library of anarchist pamphlets: *The A.B.C. of Anarchism, The Lie of Religion,* etc.

But after I had lived some months in Palestine I began
to revise my views on nationalism. I could not bring myself
to distribute the literature which was being sent. The ideas
it propagated had been dear to me, but my heart said to
me, "This is not the place for such propaganda," and I
obeyed my heart.

The well bound packages lay untouched in my basket,
and the heap kept growing. I hadn't the courage to write
my comrades not to send any more; likewise I had not the
time to sit down to a long letter of explanation. Once I
had begun work in the kitchen, I was busy night and day—
for besides the kitchen, there were my children, who went
through a good deal of sickness.

One day Brenner came into town from his colony. He
found me looking and feeling well, in spite of the work

and the hard life; and it made him happy. After some preliminary conversation he cast a glance at the packages in
the basket and asked suddenly: "What are you doing
with those books?"

"Till now I've done nothing."

"Are they going to keep on sending them to you?"

"I don't know. I haven't even acknowledged the receipt
of the first batch."

"Are you thinking of distributing them?"

I could not answer . . . Brenner understood me, and
with a smile he said:

"You'd better write them to stop sending books."

"And what about these?" I asked him.

"Oh," he said, in the same tone, "these have to be read,
of course."

"But they'll drive me out of Palestine."

"Nonsense!"

Late in the evening, after Brenner was gone, I unpacked
some pamphlets and laid them out on the reading table
in the club. The next day the club was blazing about the
"uninvited guests."

"Find the fellow, teach him a lesson, and drive him out
of Palestine." These were the comments. But I observed
that these same wild men waited for their opportunity and
slipped the forbidden literature into their pockets. Brenner
came in that evening. He sat at the long table and watched
old Halpern*, who was fanning the air with one of the
pamphlets and shouting: "Don't worry; this man'll belong
to us yet; he came to Palestine an anarchist, and he'll finish
up in harness with us."

Tel Aviv **D. A.**

---

*Michael Halpern, one of the most remarkable personalities in the Palestine
workers' movement, came to Palestine in 1886, and helped found the first
worker's organisation, in Rishon le-Zion. He was long active in the Socialist
Zionist Poale Zion party. For fifteen years he was worker and *Shomer* (guard)
in Judæa and Galilee. Died in 1919. His grave is in the Boruchov wood in
Machnaim.

THE STRIKE IN ACRE

THERE was a group of us, young women pioneers who had just landed in Palestine. Before we had had time to acclimatise ourselves, and get used to the life, we found work in the old citadel town of Acre.

Two facts were in our favor: we were new to the country and we were not yet members of the *Histadruth* (Labor Federation). The owners of the Nur match factory in Acre always preferred unorganised women workers.

The working conditions in the factory were ghastly. Many of the women received betwen five and ten piastres (twenty-five to fifty cents) a day. Sanitary conditions were unspeakable. There were no Jewish doctors. We could not make use of the *Kupat Cholim*, the labor sick fund, because the bosses did not recognise the labor organisation. Among the Arabs there were children of six and eight who were employed in the most dangerous part of the work.

There were no experienced workers among us to teach us methods of organisation. Our location cut us off from easy contact with the centre of the labor movement; but this separation also served to draw us, the workers, closer to each other; and in this closeness one ideal was nourished: we were going to build up a new Jewish settlement in this remote and abandoned town of Acre; we were going to create a new, decent life for the workers, and we were going to bring a new spirit into the lives of the Arabs in the factory. In the ancient garrison town of Acre a new kind of war now began, and blood was shed in a cause that had been unknown till our coming.

The strike broke out February 16th, 1927. The strikers

made the following demands: improvement of sanitary conditions; hiring of a Jewish doctor; some sort of payment during sickness; a fifty per cent increase in wages for workers now earning from five to ten piastres a day; an increase of twenty-five per cent to those getting ten to twenty piastres a day; children were not to be put to dangerous work. There were sixty Jewish and forty Arab strikers. The strike lasted for four months and twelve days.

I want to describe just one incident in that strike.

We had put up pickets round the factory, to prevent strike-breakers from entering. One Friday, when the last picket was about to leave, we—a group of us who had already been relieved from our posts—received a message to come back at once to the factory. Without thinking much, we set off at a run, choosing different streets so that no panic would arise among the Arabs of the city. In front of the factory we found what looked like a battle array: policemen on horseback and a huge throng round them. The workers massed themselves together, and extended in chain formation across the street. At a given signal the horsemen rushed the crowd and scattered it, leaving only the workers. These were arrested, handcuffed and led away. Only the women were left on the spot. The employer waited for the arrival of the Irish-British police to deal with these.

We were tired, so we sat down on the ground to rest. In a little while we heard the noise of automobiles—the Irish police! The officers sprang out, approached the boss, and asked him what was to be done. He told them that he was sick and tired of having us around. He wanted us removed.

We heard a whistle of command. In an instant the soldiers were let loose on us. The street became a battle-field. We were thrown to the ground and murderously beaten. Blood-stains began to show on the earth. And when we had been beaten into submission we were thrust into

the automobiles. A few women remained where they were—
they had fainted.

We were taken to the prison, and there we found the
men who had been arrested before us. The sight of us, with
hair wildly disarranged, with blood-stains on our clothes,
froze them in horror. One of our comrades could not contain himself, and began to curse the Government. An English soldier dashed at him and struck him. The girls screamed and tried to throw themselves between the two. The
noise brought officers to the scene. They ordered that we
be removed from the room, and so we were separated from
our comrades.

We were thrust in through a low, iron door which banged
to behind us; we heard the lock being turned. We looked
at each other in a sort of stupefaction, our very faces
strange to us. And sitting there we began to sing at last
the beautiful, cheering "Fisher-Song" of the *Ohel,* the
workers' theatre of Palestine.

The police returned, ordered us out of this room, and
marched us down a long corridor, on either side of which
were little cubicles. We were concentrated in one of these.
There we waited, wondering what was going to be done
with us. Meanwhile the police walked up and down, and
kept looking in on us; it was a curious sight to them—
Jewish girls in prison!

The little room became darker and darker; the sun was
setting on the other side of the walls. Comrades from the
outside were admitted to us; they brought us food and
told us that the Jewish population of Acre had organised
a protest meeting. While they were still speaking, we
heard suddenly the ringing sound of a smack—and our
comrades vanished. For a while their voices carried to
us from the outside. Silently we sat down on the floor,
around the lantern.

Chavurath ha-Poaloth, Ramath Gan.   MALCAH.

THE STRIKE IN ZICHRON JAKOB

It is two o'clock in the afternoon. Since early morning the women workers have been standing at the gate of the orchard and have stopped the strike-breakers, the Arab women and Yemenites brought down by the PICA (the Palestine Jewish Colonisation Association). Yesterday a resolution was passed in the workers' club to declare a strike against the PICA for having reduced the pay of the women workers from fifteen to ten piastres a day.

Twice we drove away the local police from the gate of the orchard. Now we are told that the next train is bringing British gendarmerie from Haifa.

Voices are heard. "Let's go away. They'll drive us off anyway. It's three o'clock. Tomorrow morning we'll come back early."

But opposing voices are louder: "No! No! We'll not go away of our own free will. The moment we go, the strike-breakers will get in. Let's stay."

The strikers' committee is in session. Messages fly back and forth between the meeting and the group of women at the orchard gate. We wait for the decision of the committee.

The decision is: Stay on!

Here they come—the British soldiers with an officer at their head. The conversation with the officer was a waste of time. He tried to argue with the women pickets at the gate, and with the men workers who stood at a distance. (They, not being directly involved, had to stand to one side, as "onlookers.")

We were given fifteen minutes to think the matter over. But we only closed our ranks, one behind the other, to guard the gate. The fifteen minutes passed, and then the soldiers, who had been standing woodenly at attention advanced on the workers and began to strike them with the butts of their rifles. The women screamed—but they stood still closer together. Who were these assailants? British soldiers in Palestine, called out by the PICA against women who were struggling for a bare means of subsistence! The first row of the women held out in front, near the men who had come to their help. The last row of women clung firm about the gate.

How long can a group of unarmed men and women hold out against English soldiers? The first line shuddered and began to yield. The rifles flashed up and down, broke the strikers, pursued them. . .

Our turn next—our. last row of women.

I hear a trembling voice near me. "I'm frightened."

"If you're frightened, leave! Leave at once! We don't want to be told that we were scared of English soldiers."

"Don't talk like that to me! Give me strength."

Again the officer came up.

"Wouldn't you do better to submit this whole matter to the High Commissioner?"

The answer comes from the group. "We won't leave this gate."

In spite of that determined answer, the officer still gives us five minutes in which to think it over. He stands in front of us and waits. But in our minds there is only one question: Will we have the courage and the strength to put up a fight, not to run when they advance on us? It is the first time that we clash with the police. It is not the orchard gate we are defending, and not only our crust of bread— we are defending our pride! If only these five minutes would pass! We press each other's hands feverishly, we jam ourselves closer about the gate. And now the line of soldiers comes at us—civilized Englishmen with guns in their hands, setting on women! There is a smile on their faces, as though the whole incident were something of unusual interest. And it is this smile which burns deeper than anything else. They try to break through, to open the gate, they pull savagely at the women—but we hold firm. Their comrades come to their help.

I find myself suddenly hanging in the air between Englishmen and comrades. Two soldiers are pulling at me, and cannot get me loose. A third joins them. I have only one prayer in my heart—not to let go. A feeling of hatred wells up in me for those blue-green eyes and that blue-green uniform.

But in the end they smashed through, and I was flung to one side, to be surrounded by the local police. I got up and tried to return to the struggling mass at the gate. Again I was seized and flung back. The officer was no better than his men—they belong to one level of culture . . . Behind the guard stand the arrested men, tied to each other in one long chain. Out of the struggle we smile at them—the smile of friendship and encouragement shining across a sea of hatred and rage.

At last the gate was opened. The arrested men were led off to Zichron, and the women workers dragged after them. That night we ran through the streets of the colony, crying: "Liberate them! Liberate them!" We bloodied our hands beating on the door of the temporary prison in which our comrades were locked. We sacked the office of the PICA, and left it turned upside down. And we quieted down only when our comrades were set free.

Kinereth: Group of ha-Shomer ha-Tzair.   CARMELAH.

FIGHTING FOR WORK

THIS is the first day of our imprisonment here.*
I remember well how they lifted us, bound hand and
foot, into the automobiles. We managed to gasp out words
of farewell to our comrades who remained there on the
the "battlefield"— and then everything disappeared.

My side ached. My face was burning, and there were
tears in my eyes—but they were tears of rage.

We did not know where the automobiles were taking us,
to the colony or to the prison in Jaffa. We were not accustomed to being bound like that, and as the machines rolled
on we tried now and again to move our limbs. Yet we could
not help laughing through our tears. Automobiles and
groups of workers passed us on the road, and we saluted
them by shaking the manacles on our hands.

The passersby stared at us in fright—they could not
understand what had happened. We passed through Tel
Aviv, and were recognised by acquaintances. They called
to us: "Where are they taking you?" One of the women
in our car shouted back: "For a stroll on the sea-shore."
And she was almost right! Here we were driving through
the narrow streets of Jaffa and the sea burst on our view.

The automobile drives into the police yard; we are taken
out and forced into a small room, and from there we issue
again into the yard. High walls surround us. On a rug sits
a Yemenite woman, and three Arab women near her. The
woman guard and the others are anxious to find out why

---

*In the winter of 1927 the Jewish workers of Petach Tikvah put up a fierce
struggle for their right to be employed in the orange picking. In the course
of the struggle there was a clash between strikers and police, and the former
were brutally treated. The incident stirred the entire Jewish world.

we have been brought here. We answer that we wanted work, and we got . . . we show them the blood spots on our dresses. We ask the Yemenite woman why the Arabs are here. She answers: "For stealing."

The day passes, and we sit there on rugs, feeling as though our limbs have been smashed. The police come in, leisurely, at ease. They take our names and go away. They have plenty of time.

It grows dark. We are led back into the prison—a tiny, whitewashed room, with a tile floor and an electric lamp— a charming home! We lay the rugs and blankets on the floor, and lie down close to each other, tired out as if after a day's work. The woman guard brings food for the prisoners, a gruel in a tin cup, and a loaf of black bread. For us she has white bread, eggs and oranges.

"Where's this from?"

"Your comrades brought it."

Who was it? The Federation? We had not expected it; we had forgotten that we were bound up with an entire world which was following our fate closely.

We woke up the next morning realising for the first time that we were really in prison. And yet, in spite of the prohibition, we got the newspapers. When the woman guard went out we fell on those papers like hungry wolves on meat. We read wildly, too impatient to follow the text sentence by sentence. We want to get all the news at one glance.

We learn now that the entire labor body of the country stands with us. We seem to have done something! If it brings no results here and now, there is hope that results will follow. In any case, we have focussed the attention of the country on our case. Oh, it was worth while! We can hardly remember another moment of such joy and satisfaction.

They brought us mail to the prison, and I received a postal card from my home, back in Europe. My father wrote that one sister had been sent to Siberia for being "counter-revolutionary." And here I was in prison for being too revolutionary! Another sister, so my father wrote, "lives in loneliness, one Jewess among many Gentiles."

I read and read and repeat the words.

"To be a daughter of the Jewish people means, to be faithful far away among strangers, and to be a stranger at home among one's own."

Chavurath ha-Poaloth in Petach Tikvah.   REBECCAH.

DESTRUCTION

From the Riots of August, 1929

IT WAS on Friday evening, August 23rd, 1929, that the comrades came back from the Nesher cement factory outside Haifa to guard our settlement, that we learned what had happened in Jerusalem.

The night passed peacefully. When the sun rose the next morning we somehow felt more light-hearted. The comrades returned to the Nesher factory, and we went out into the fields.

A few hours later our watchman, Eliezer Hurwitz, was called to Haifa to the workers' council. They told him that we would have to leave the place because it was rumored that the riots were going to spread from Jerusalem over the entire country. Our place was far from town, closed in by the hills, and near by was an Arab village which was known to be a centre of disturbance; it would be hard to afford us protection. After a long conference we decided not to leave the place, for we knew that, once it was abandoned, it would be completely destroyed.

We explained this to our comrades of the Nesher, who stood guard with us the second night too. They pleaded with us to give up our decision; the situation throughout the whole country was dangerous and, empty-handed as they were, it would be impossible for them to defend our settlement in case of attack.

Sunday morning the same thing—again the demand from Haifa that we abandon the position; again we reply, "Send help so that we can defend the place." Meanwhile we make what preparation we can. On the distant road we see the automobiles of the Arabs flying back and forth. There are rumors of an impending attack in Haifa.

At five o'clock two automobiles come from the Nesher, and now the men speak determinedly: "The place has to be abandoned." We feel now that argument is useless. With heavy hearts we begin to pack things into the automobiles. I go into the shed to get the cow, and there stands one of my comrades; she and I lower our eyes, and the thought goes through us simultaneously: "So much labor we put into this place, so much suffering—and now everything is to go up in smoke."

We caught the chickens, bound them, and placed them in the machines. A couple of packages contained our clothes. Meanwhile the men stood impatiently by and urged us on. "Faster!" Darkness begins to creep up. The haste, the tumult, the screaming of the fowl—everything confuses us and runs into a pandemonium. We are ready now, the automobiles are about to start, and something new turns up. The watchman refuses to get in! "I don't leave this place," he says, obstinately. "It's my job to stay here and see it isn't destroyed." The moment we hear these words, we make an effort to clamber out of the cars, saying: "If he stays, we stay." But it's too late. The comrades give the signal to the chauffeur and the machines are off.

It was a fearful night that we passed in Haifa. We could scarcely wait for the dawn. As soon as it was light we got into the first automobile we could commandeer and drove back at top speed to the settlement. When we saw, in the distance, the watchman standing at the door of the dining-room, a load fell off our hearts.

Once we were at the settlement, we were also without news from Haifa, for Jewish automobiles no longer passed up the road. For the same reason, we could not return to the Nesher factory. We settled down to the usual routine of work. At eight in the morning we observed a crowd of Arab men and women, numbering between thirty and forty, approaching us. They were armed with clubs. At the hedge they came to a halt and, after a pause, began to make for the gate. But they did not seem to be united. There seemed to be quarreling among them; we saw the Arab women trying to pull the men away from the gate. And indeed, the crowd retired a little from the hedge and stood there, yelling and pointing at us. Before long three Arab automobiles arrived. One of them turned toward the Arab village, the other went on to Haifa, and the third stopped with the crowd.

And now our watchman perceived that things were getting bad and that we would have done better to stay in Haifa. He was beside himself with remorse, but it was too late. There was nowhere to run to! To go out upon the road would be to deliver ourselves up. And once again the watchman became obstinate—but this time at the other extreme. "It's my fault that you came back here!" he exclaimed. "I'm going out of here! I'll find my way to the Nesher and have them send an automobile." We implored him not to jeopardise his life, but he paid no attention to us. He saddled the horse and set out at a gallop. We saw him disappear, and our hearts told us that we would not see him alive again. When the Arabs saw him ride off, they drew closer and began to yell: "Clear out of this place! If you don't, you'll be cut to pieces."

Twenty minutes of horror passed. We locked ourselves in the dining-room, the only building with stone walls, and waited there, pale, helpless. And we read in each other's eyes the question which had no answer: "How will we defend ourselves? What with?"

It seemed to us that hours, unusually long hours, had passed since the watchman had set out. And then, at last, we heard the shrill, liberating whistle—the comrades of the Nesher had arrived in an automobile.

We still had to pass through the Arab village, and we wondered if we would be able to get through. The road passed by the Sheikh's house. In front of it the whole village had gathered, and the Sheikh sat on a white horse, delivering an address. A crowd of young people had detached itself, and was waiting for our car, and as we flew by, a hail of stones came crashing round the automobile We got through safely; in the Nesher factory they received us as if we had been dragged back alive from the grave.

Two aeroplanes circled above the village, firing at random to disperse the Arabs.

The guards were doubled in the Nesher. The women were now installed for the night. We could not rest. We kept staring in the direction of our home, waiting for the inevitable—for the flames and smoke.

Nothing was observed in the night. At noon of the next day, however, a column of smoke rises from that corner of the horizon. From the roof of the factory we can just make out that the Arabs have set fire to the hayrick. The barracks are intact. The hayrick blazes, and we begin to hope that this will be the sum total of the damage.

But at midnight a wild blaze colored all that part of the sky. The barracks. . .

We become frantic. We implore the men: "Quick: let's go back. Perhaps we can put the fire out." Always we get the same answer. "Can't do a thing. We have no weapons. And we have to guard the Nesher first."

We stand there paralysed, and watch the blaze. So much labor, so much love and sacrifice! All of it going up in the flames.

An automobile with English soldiers comes rushing up to the factory. They tell us in detail what has happened at the farm, what is burning and what has been destroyed. But they cannot take us there.

Early in the morning we asked the four Englishmen who had been sent to defend the Nesher, to take us over to the farm. They agreed. We arrived in the midst of a deathly silence, a desolation that appalled us. This has been our home for the last three years! Nothing at all is left of the barracks; only the ribs of the iron beds stick out gruesomely from the ruin. The store-room is empty; fragments of the smashed incubator lie scattered on the ground. We take

a look at the tree nursery. Eveything is green and fresh
and undisturbed. We breathe once more. The ruffians did
not understand at all that for us the nursery means everything, that it is more important than the barracks.

The English soldiers grow impatient. We must leave.
But how hard it is to tear ourselves away from here.

And, sitting in the automobiles, we begin to make plans
for getting back the same day in order to water the young
trees.

Chavurath ha-Poaloth near Haifa.   SARAH.

PART III
AT WORK

III

AT WORK

STAGES

FROM the beginning of her appearance in the country twenty-five years ago, the woman worker has been closely bound up with the general labor movement; and yet the ways of the women workers are peculiar to themselves.

Even at the outset, when workers took their first grip on the land, in the days of the first *kvutzoth*—Sedjera, Deganiah, Kinereth and Merchaviah—days of triumph for the workers' ideals, even in those days some of the women workers had already separated off into a special women's *kvutzah* or commune, a *kvutzah* without a home, a wandering *kvutzah* which had neither soil nor plan nor budget.

What brought this thing about?

In the thick of that passionate movement toward the land the women workers suddenly found themselves thrust aside and relegated once more to the ancient tradition of the house and the kitchen. They were amazed and disappointed to see how the cleavage was opening, the men comrades really uniting themselves with the land, but they, though on it, not becoming part of it. The united front was cracking. So that even then a handful of women—all of them very young—set out in a group to build up their own working relationship to the soil.

And quickly enough there began to spring up those early *kvutzoth* of women workers—on the shore of Galilee, in the Emek (the Valley of Jezreel) and on the sands of Judaea. And if the *kvutzah* subsisted only for one year,

and if the land it worked was only hired—who cared?
For the principle issue was not the farm, the economic
unit, but the *kvutzah* as such. Nor did they find it so hard
to break in the naked soil of the wilderness, if thereby they
could slake their thirst for work on the land, and satisfy
their passion for a partnership with mother earth.

There was much joking about those early *kvutzoth*. No
one believed in the success of our idea. But the deep, burning enthusiasm which had caught us up enabled us to ignore the doubts of others. Yes, it is quite clear now to
everyone that the temporary *kvutzah* was *economically
senseless*. But in those days it had a deep sense, and because of this it emerged whole from the difficult war period.

Shortly before the close of the war the dream of a Jewish
Legion ripened into realisation. The woman worker was
caught up in that rush of sacrifice not less than the man;
what the *kvutzah* had not been able to satisfy in her, she
sought to fulfil in this new phenomenon. It is not easy to
write about those sacrificial days. Were the women really
caught up in a military emotion—or were they merely imi-
tating the men comrades? No, no. That spirit was absent
on both sides. We were enslaved by one idea; one well
of feeling sent up its deep, turbulent forces in both of us;
the idea was not war, but liberation. But for the men
there was the front—and for the women, again, disappointment. There were hundreds of women who reported for
duty with the Legion, just like men. Of course, they were
not taken. That rebuff left us flat and wearied; *we* were
not to participate in that great moment. This incident
deserves a place of its own in the history of the women
workers' movement.

The year after the war those girls' *kvutzoth* disappeared;
it was something sudden, as if a sponge had wiped them
off the slate. Nor was there any struggle about it. The
women felt that this form had outlived itself; something
new had to answer the spirit of the changed times. Yes,
we could no longer form our associations so easily, wander

from place to place, take root and uproot every year. The time had come for the permanent settlement, stable, rooted in its own soil.

After the wandering *kvutzah* came, as its natural inheritor, the *meshek ha-Poaloth,* the women's training farm; after group vagabondage came the planned, sensible and stabilised unit.

And so the women's farm was created in Petach Tikvah, the tree nursery in Jerusalem, and the collectives in Nachlath Jehudah and Shechunath Boruchov.

This was in nineteen twenty-one, the time of the big expansion in agricultural work, when the Emek was bought and new forms of land units sprang up, the large *kvutzoth,* or communes, the *moshav ovdim,* or workers' individualist-cooperative settlement. In every place the woman worker had her own important role to play.

It does not matter what the exact forces were which brought about the result, whether it was through the pressure of the original women's farms, or through the actual necessities of the life on the land—but as a worker the woman found her role to be richer, fuller and more variegated than ever before. Her place was definite: the vegetable gardening system, the dairy work, chicken-raising and tree-planting. She was gradually relieved from the exclusive claim of the kitchen and laundry; the men learned to give her a hand there. But once she broke into the fuller life of the system, the woman began to understand how much she lacked in training and independent preparation.

A new and complicated question emerged: the question of mother and child in the workers' collectives. The woman began anxiously to seek a way to unite care of the child with productive labor on the soil. And out of this search arose new life-forms in the field of child-rearing. If we have been enriched by many values in this field, we must thank the woman worker on the land.

Another period came—the time when thousands of Palestinian Jews were taken up with the road-building which was a feature of certain after-war years. Among these road-laborers were women, too, participating, but often at a loss as to the meaning of this participation, doubtful of themselves and of their new role.

The body of workers in Palestine grew constantly, and the number of women workers with it; but most of these were still employed in their own separate settlements or else were wage-workers in the villages. The mother in the worker's farm and the daughter in the farm settlement of women workers still have more in common than the mother in the village and the daughter in the town—the land-work is a bond. And this question of the relation between mother and child plays as important a part in our conferences and our conversations as the questions of work and of immigration into Palestine.

The *meshek ha-poaloth,* or women's farm settlement, has a distinct purpose: to prepare the woman worker for the general *meshek* or farm settlement. But at first it had an additional purpose: it was a larger school life. There was an educational value in the dividing up of the work, the sharing of responsibility and the adaptation of the individual to the group life. The *meshek* had to be self-supporting; and therefore the comrades in it had to take up all its economic problems. In such surroundings the character of the woman comrade set firm; she developed the necessary independence and initiative. We were amazed sometimes to see the difference which one year made in a woman. Helpless at first, she was at the end of this period an intelligent cooperator, participating in the management and showing a thorough understanding of the complicated economic and administrative problems of the settlement.

Work in the settlement was a joy. Steeped as we were in our labors, the hours of the long day slipped by uncounted and unnoticed. But the purest and most supreme joy was in the tree nurseries—our pioneer contribution to the country.

In old Europe and in new America, which possess such magnificent agricultural institutions, and even in California with its nurseries which number their shoots by the million, it is always the man who directs. Managers, gardeners, workers—all men—are the creative and responsible elements. The woman worker is hardly to be seen. Here and there I found a few women wage-workers, or office-workers—in brief, they were given the inferior or mechanical work, which dulls the individual. Not one single tree nursery did I find created by women.

With our own hands we raised, on our soil, tens and hundreds of thousands of shoots, and a kind of bond was created between our fruitful little corners and the wild, bare hills around us. We were participants in the great task of re-afforesting the country.

But we share in something more than in the forestry. We play a role in gardening, chicken-raising and dairy work. It is true that these activities have not yet taken deep, organic root among us. They still lack something; here we are short of a breed cow, there the barn is not completed; elsewhere we lack buildings, or soil—or even water; and nearly everywhere we are short of quarters for the workers. The universal trouble is that the settlement has not yet established itself on its own feet.

The critical years 1926-1927 came upon us. Everywhere, unemployment, hunger and suffering—and most of all among the women workers. The women farm settlements knew all the bitterness of those years. So many women workers came knocking at our doors—and there was no way of admitting them. The settlements were still small, their absorptive capacity was limited. Two hundred women in the settlements had food and genuine creative work; two thousand outside of them were hungry and without employment. And among the latter one heard dark, bitter remarks about the *meshek*—the darling women's institution, which picks and chooses and accords its privileges according to its own rules. . .

Out of this suffering came creation. The *meshek*, the women's training farm, gave birth to the *chavurah*. The idea was born among the comrades in the *meshek*, and they transformed it into a reality.

The *meshek* is still young—and it has its special needs. There is, for instance, the tree nursery. How much labor, how much attention, must be put into that enterprise, year in, year out, creating and re-creating! The worry about water, the care which must be given to every individual plant and sapling! And then the worries of selling them. . . The *meshek* absorbs the woman worker wholly, body and soul. But if the woman feels herself fitted for this work she gives herself up gladly and unreflectingly.

But the heaviest strain on the *meshek* is the constant round of women who come and go. So much effort must be expended before the new comrade gets into harness, and before she adapts herself to the group life. And when the two years have passed, and the "course" is completed— she goes, and the *meshek* begins all over again with another new-comer. This in itself, apart from the agricultural, the "real" work, is an exacting task, and it is little wonder that the years plough so deeply into the faces of the women who direct the settlements.

And then new changes come up in the realities of Palestine. Factories and workshops rise in these towns. Thousands of women pour into the cities and go into the factory or into private homes; and during those same years, 1926-1928, the country is closed to Jewish immigration.

Just yesterday there were hundreds knocking at the door of the *meshek*s and suddenly we are short of hands! And those women whose lives have been sunk in these institutions feel as if a blow had struck at them. Something must be done. Out of the new needs come new ideals: the *meshek* must *give* more. It must be perfected from within. Everyone of its agricultural enterprises must become a model. It is, after all, an institution which educates and trains. And then other problems must be settled, worked out to better ends: markets, the inner form of life in the institution, improvements in the theory and practice of teaching. But all these things are external compared with the fundamental problem of the woman worker herself, and of her attitude toward the *meshek*. True, the *meshek* is a training ground, but it must not be regarded merely as an institution where women come to learn a trade. It is not a trade, it is a sort of personal destiny we teach. . . . The woman learns to educate herself, and to awaken from within a deep and permanent relationship to the soil.

The development of the women's *meshek* was naturally influenced by the general conditions in the labor movement.

We, the women of the *meshek*, are particularly proud of one fact: our accepted and accredited public workers also take up the physical labor and are swallowed up by it. As soon as they go on the soil they forget their public or communal occupation and become one with the actual labor itself. And many of them are now spread through the collectives of the Emek, the Jordan and Kinereth, in the women's settlements and at many another point. This characteristic of so many women leaders, their ability to sink their public careers in sheer physical work, is often pointed to with pride among us, as a sign of a certain superiority over men. But it is possible that the ability is rooted in passivity, in an absence of courage and a weaker taste for public work.

In fact, how else can we explain the fact that we have achieved so little among the women workers in the city?

Hundreds and thousands of women belonging to the older Jewish settlement in Palestine, women of all classes and ages, are pouring into factories, toward the sewing machine and loom, and even into domestic service—and at what wretched pay! And so many of them are not at all organised, have no membership in the Federation.

The basements in the side streets of the towns swarm with workers' families. In Jerusalem—and principally

there—the worker families live mostly among the Oriental
Jews. The family suffers as a whole, but it is the working
class mother that suffers most. And if any child needs the
upbringing which is found in the collectives, it is that city
child of the worker. What joy it would be for that mother,
what a blessing for the child, if a workers' settlement could
be founded for them somewhere outside the city, a little
patch of earth begging to be worked. Why is it then that
no movement has been started among the women workers
for such settlements?

And one point more, about wage work in the colonies.
However difficult it is for the men to find jobs, insecure as
these jobs are—yet they have made a place for themselves
in every branch of agriculture, in the plantations and fields.
But the woman still has to fight out the problem of her right
to work in the colony, in the orchard and vineyard; and
not merely at the picking of oranges. And how few women
get a man's pay for doing a man's work!

Out of this rises doubt, and dissatisfaction and inade-
quacy; in the workers' settlement, the *kvutzah*, the individualist colony—everywhere the woman feels the same. In
no form of Palestinian life does the woman play her proper
role economically, culturally and spiritually.

The road which lies before the women in Palestine is
still a long one, but its direction already seems to be clear:
however strong our desire to broaden the basis of woman's
life in village and town, so as to make it all-inclusive, *the
directive principle is and must remain, for the entire women
workers' movement, agricultural.*

To leave out agriculture is to leave out the most vital part
of the labor movement in Palestine; to take away the
meshek ha-Poaloth, the settlement of the women workers,
is to take away from the woman labor movement its chief
and characteristic productivity.

Meshek ha-Poaloth in
    Jerusalem   RACHEL JANAITH.

IN THE KVUTZAH

In regard to the *kvutzah* we have developed an attitude which is altogether too much like that of the nagging mother toward her children—an attitude of unceasing criticism. There seems to be no limit to the demands that we make on the group and on the individual—as if the *kvutzah* were already the perfected form of life in a perfected social system of the future. From the individual we demand that he be a good worker, disciplined, devoted, filled with a sense of responsibility, open and accessible to his comrades. From the *kvutzah* we demand that it shall satisfy all the material and spiritual needs of the individual.

We forget that in the existing order of things, with its competitive character, men and women are brought up to be enemies. We who have gone into the *kvutzoth* have taken a leap into the future; we have refused to wait, but must incorporate the best that is to come in our own lives. But we cannot leap out of our skins; and we cannot cast off with one gesture all the heritage of our early training and be reborn. We are still the same persons. And the many comrades who yield to despair because we are not perfect are only the victims of an exaggerated idealism.

Why are we so prone to pass over the good element in our life? We have so much to say about its shortcomings —is there nothing to be said for its achievements? There are enough good points in our own life (and how many more in the life of our children!) to justify a little praise, a corrective to the monotonously one-sided and misleading self-criticism in which we indulge.

We were very young when we came into the country. We knew nothing about life, and nothing of the prosaic

side of men and women. Our group contacts had always
been festive: we saw each other during visits, during out-
ings, and on those occasions when the youth-movement
brought us together. We were friends and comrades, and
each of us worried for the others. Little wonder that in
those days we thought that all human beings were good.

But it is otherwise in the actual life of the *kvutzah*. Here
we come into intimate contact (I will not say that our
knowledge of each other is intimate) and it is inevitable
that we should also learn of each other's shortcomings—
human shortcomings which are even apt to eclipse the
greatest virtues.

There is a special feature in *kvutzah* life which goes under
the heading of "being good." To "be good" means, with
us, to be faithful and responsible in the work. In the one
case it may be the heart which supplies the impulse; in the
other it may be a highly developed sense of duty. The result is, however, the same. Such a person is "a good worker." Not that the phrase is frequently used; more often
than not we simply accept it as something natural and
self-understood. That is what we are here for.

And in the same way we are actually unconscious of the
concept "mutual help" because we work together all day
long, and the process itself is one of mutual help. We fail to
remember, in our fits of self-criticism, even those cases of
exceptional and generous mutual help which occur in our
life.

Here is one instance. There are few things which make
a new mother more unhappy than the failure of her own
supply of milk for her baby. In the *kvutzah* it is a simple and
accepted custom, in such cases, that one mother shall help
another, and mothers feed the children of others with
the same devotion as their own. If one who is capable of
doing this should show signs of discontent—let alone re-
fuse!—she would never be forgiven. On one occasion, I remember, a woman happened to forget to feed a comrade's
baby, and, when she recollected suddenly, she ran through

rain and mud down the long road to the children's house. But we say nothing about such things. We find them natural; and in any case we see no reason to make any particular fuss about decent moral behavior.

Our "peasant," who gets up in seeding time at four o'clock in the morning, and does not return till late in the evening—is he less devoted than the man who tills a field which is his own? The woman who cooks for dozens, or for hundreds of men—is she less concerned, less thoughtful, than if she were cooking for her own family? And have we not ourselves admitted that there is something wonderful about our women who work in our nurseries, our children's houses, and make themselves one with their charges? Is there not in all this an influence which lifts the individual above those meaner concepts of "advancement", of "getting on in the world" on which he has been brought up? As for those of our comrades who are taken up with the public work, and who know no rest night or day—do we treat them with the respect which is their due? And if we do not—does that prevent them from carrying on?

We complain sometimes of the lack of friendliness; we fail to visit, let us say, a sick comrade. The truth is that we are usually so exhausted that we are unable to summon up energy for an evening with friends. Apart from this, we are with the crowd all day long, and in the evenings we feel the longing to withdraw a little into ourselves, to rest, to read.

In life at large the most typical sin of the individual is his attitude of carelessness toward public property. In organised society the utmost ingenuity is needed, on the part of a state or city government, to protect its possessions. It seems to be almost instinctive in the individual to be prodigal with public property, even when he gets no benefit himself. I remember how, in Russia, there was, during the war, a great shortage of electricity. But you could not persuade the people to conserve. Lights would be left burning all night—what's the difference? This blind destructiveness of "anonymous" values lives in almost every human being. Can this be said of us? And is it not true that even in the last few years there has been a great advance in this respect among all our groups?

There are some who complain that our children are "dry," "formal"—"they lack the softness and gentle-heartedness that we used to have as children." These people forget the virtues which *our* children have, and which *we* lacked as children: the being accustomed to work, the discipline with regard to the group, the sense of responsibility with regard to tasks, the strong love of nature, a strong, authentic love, without the sentimentalism of the past.

We simply do not know how fortunate we are in our children. We hear the complaint, "The children are too cheeky!" But do we pause to distinguish between spiritual freedom, forthrightness and strength, on the one hand, and "cheek" on the other? Are not some of our concepts a trifle conservative?

And there are others who find fault even with the affirmative side of our group-rearing of children. They complain that we actually give up too much time to the children. The collective life gives the parents a certain amount of time each day to devote exclusively to their children. The child thus feels that the parents are concerned only with him; he is never "in the way." And this, too, is a bad thing!

Of course it would be absurd to say that in the *kvutzah* everything is good. But what is at fault is not the *kvutzah* as a form of life, but certain indirect factors. It is our poverty that is at fault, and our constant exhaustion. We are poor; we are unable to meet even the minimum demands of the individual, and this is the source of our discontent.

Our ideal is that everyone shall get according to his needs. Actually, because of the perpetual shortage, this essential equality is transformed into a formal, external equality. For instance: we serve out food in equal portions! The boy and the girl, the worker in the field and the light worker, all get the same. And when shall we be able to get rid of this formal equality? Only when we shall have got rid of our poverty.

Our poverty oppresses the individual, makes it impossible for him to satisfy his personal needs in accordance with his own appetite and taste. The heavy work, the constant tiredness, the blazing heat, the poor food, the life in tents and barracks, the impossibility of taking one decent rest in the course of the year, to refresh oneself with a sight of the world—these are the real causes of our dark moods and our bitterness.

But life will not always be like this for us. Houses will be built, our returns will improve, the work will become easier—and life will be easier, too.

Let us therefore be cautious in our criticisms. Our life is too difficult, too complicated. There are many short-comings to be overcome, many shadows to be removed—but let us understand the good things, too, and appreciate them.

Ain Charod   LILIA BASEVITCH.

THE WOMAN IN THE *MOSHAV OVDIM*

IT WAS in 1921 that there appeared in Palestine the form of settlement called the *moshav ovdim*—the individualist cooperative settlement, where the worker owned his own land, but could not exploit the labor of others, and where a high degree of cooperation developed. At this time of writing (1928) it is hard to say: What has the *moshav ovdim* meant for the woman? Only a few observations can be made.

The woman and her husband enter the *moshav ovdim*, and the work divides itself automatically between them. The man works in the field, far from the home, and directs the entire business; she works in and around the house. This is not a strict division. When the wife is not tied to little children, she often works by the side of her husband in the fields; and, *per contra,* he is sometimes to be found "at home" in the vegetable garden and round the chicken coop. But on the whole the direction of the home is in the woman's hands. It appears to me that this division is natural and right; and it is only when either the man or woman is constantly overworked, and the yield is not enough to keep the family, that suffering appears. But this question of increasing the productivity of agriculture in Palestine, so that it shall exact fewer human sacrifices, is a national, and not a woman's question.

As long as the woman in the *moshav* is a mother of young children, she can do very little for the farm. At best she can look after the few chickens, and attend to the tiny vegetable plot. But I have noticed that even when I have not the time to do the actual work, I feel I must at least take one look every day at the garden, if only to see whether the shoots I planted a while ago are already coming up.

A woman must be exceptionally talented to be able to grasp clearly all the problems of a large farm; but on the little family farm the ordinary woman can feel herself quite at home. And for me the principal advantage of the *moshav* is, that it gives the woman a chance to feel free and to live her own life. More than this, the *moshav* forces a certain independence on the woman. It brings the woman directly face to face with life itself, and there is nothing to shield her from the contact with hard reality.

It is true that the woman in the *moshav* pays heavily for her independence. Her burden is heavy—but we ought to understand that the carrying of a life-burden does not necessarily mean oppression, any more than comfort necessarily means freedom.

The source of our suffering is this: that the yield is not yet proportionate to our labor. Although we have overstrained ourselves—and perhaps because of it—we still cannot satisfy the most essential needs. It is true that part of the explanation lies in the conditions which have reigned and still reign in the country; but part of it lies, perhaps, in our own lack of skill and experience. For we are the first generation of Jewish land-workers here. And if it were possible to work only eight or ten hours a day, like our comrades in the towns, that alone might make the life of the woman in the *moshav* tolerable.

But of course not all women face the same circumstances. Where the children are a little older, and already attend school, the woman can go peacefully about more specific and more systematic work. A certain fine calm pervades the home life, and it can be said simply that there are families in the *moshav* which would provide an artist with an authentic idyll of the Jewish village. But where the woman must still tend little ones, there life is hard. She does not know a moment's freedom during the day, and she is never permitted to sleep the night through. She gets up at dawn, and does not know where to begin first—to feed the children or the chickens. In the majority of cases, there is not money enough in hand to lay in a stock of provisions, either for the family, or for the chickens and cattle; and so every other day the woman must go to the cooperative store, and take her turn in the line. And sometimes she must go to the clinic with her child, and there again is a line ahead of her.

Perhaps the morning passes this way; noon arrives and the noonday meal is not yet ready. And if the husband stays in the fields through the day, the woman still has to milk the cow and carry the milk away to the cooperative dairy. Sometimes she has to make a choice: if she gives her children the attention they need, she must neglect the garden and the cows—and the economy suffers; and if she attends to the economy, it is her children who must suffer.

When we first entered the *moshav,* we imagined it would make things easier if the youngest children were brought up together. But after living seven years in the *moshav* we have come to the conclusion that for us it is an impossible plan. In the *kvutzah* the children are under the care of a comrade; we, however, would have to employ a trained teacher, for it is obvious that no woman could be asked to separate herself from her own farm and do the child work. In the *kvutzah* the payment consists largely of the produce which is grown on the spot; in addition there is a little money expense for other necessities. But in the *moshav* the pay would have to be in cash, on the scale fixed by the Federation of Labor. This additional expense would be beyond the means of the woman in the *moshav*—and what she would gain in being liberated from the upbringing of the little ones, she would perhaps more than lose in additional labor.

Something else must be borne in mind. At the outset, when the farm is just being established, the woman in the *moshav* gets hardly any directly productive work. As long as the irrigation system is not installed, and the chicken-coops are not built, there is, naturally plenty of work, hard work for the woman; but she earns next to nothing. And when the years have passed, and the farm has developed somewhat, and the woman adapts herself to the new life—then she suddenly perceives that the general group expenses are very high; and most of the comrades in the *moshav* are in debt to the council for taxes. And this being the case, the group education of the little ones, expensive as it is, becomes a mere dream. Moreover, there are many women on the *moshav* who are opposed on principle to the group education of the very young.

The conditions under which the woman in the *moshav* works are exceptionally hard. No one would dream of telling a man to work the fields without a plough or to set up a dairy without a shed. But a woman is expected to raise chickens when she has neither a chicken yard nor a coop. How much energy is lost that way? The woman goes out to feed the chickens—but first she must search them out in neighboring yards. She sows and plants in a yard without a fence, and chicken and cattle trample the beds, and undo all her work. She washes her laundry under a burning sun, without a roof above her and without the proper vessels. She bakes the bread in a primitive oven. How much useless suffering we could spare her if we understood that the economy of the home is entitled to the same systematisation as the economy of the field.

What becomes of the woman in such circumstances? She is perpetually enslaved, perpetually under the heavy yoke; she has no time to enjoy a book—no time even for the Labor Daily. It is true, too, that the men in the *moshav* cannot indulge themselves in the luxury of sitting down to a book; they too are in constant harness. But men have had a better education in their boyhood, and this helps to carry them through the later years. Most of our comrades learned the Hebrew language and its literature in their childhood, and when they arrived in Palestine felt themselves at home in the new culture.

But in the case of the woman her ignorance in this field

not only hinders her from adapting herself to the life of Palestine, but it also overshadows her relation to her children. She is not simply "occupied" with her children, she is completely sunk in them. The man, however faithful he be to his children and his farm, has only to shake them off in order to be free, and then he can easily take up public or cultural interests. He re-unites himself with them as if he had never known the physical slavery of his farm.

And in this respect there is, I think, little difference between the woman in the *moshav* and the woman in the *kvutzah*. Whether she brings up her children herself, or sends them into the group under the care of the teacher, she is still a woman and a mother. But I sometimes believe that if a woman entered her own family life with a richer spiritual and educational equipment she would not, later, as a mother, feel herself so completely sundered from the world at large.

One more point I want to touch: mutual help among the women of the *moshav*. I have observed that it is the women with little children who soon become used up. When such women are compelled to go away to a hospital, or a rest home, the problem arises: Who will take care of the children? As a rule our mutual aid consists in the fact that when a woman is ill, the neighbors will take turns looking after the children. But when it is a question of a protracted illness, this sort of help is inadequate. Then the mutual aid committee is compelled to hire, at its own expense, an outside person. But this is not the right way out. In the first place, the children suffer under this arrangement; in the second, we are averse to using hired help.

For cases of this kind a common children's house would be the right thing. Such a house should be constructed by the Central Workers' Hospital in the Emek, and the various Committees of Mutual Aid in the *moshavim* should contribute to its support. It is up to the Councils of Women Workers to work out the plan for this institution and to place it before interested circles.

The years will pass, our children will grow up, the farms will develope—and then life will be easier. Out of our sons and daughters will be built the Jewish family, rooted deep in its own soil. And then many of those problems which leave us helpless today will be answered of themselves.

Nahalal   SHOSHANA RECHTHANT-JAFFA.

IN NAHALAL

WHEN I look back on these last seven years—the years of my life in the settlement of Nahalal—I am aware of no striking or outstanding incident; the only thing that has happened is that human labor has made something out of nothing. I remember the sand-dunes used to grow along the lake at home—hillock added to hillock. So my life has grown here, one hillock of labor after another, an economy with its own form and content, a family with its own tradition. Perhaps we all exaggerate when we speak about our past, yet I must say that in these seven years in Nahalal I did not for one moment forget that I was a wife, a mother and the director of a household, an economic unit.

Nahalal is founded on the family; this is the inner being of the place. It may seem fantastic that people should be erecting a new structure on a foundation which is already shaky. And yet the life of Nahalal does not swallow up the personality of the woman; on the contrary, it strengthens and confirms it.

The form of our village is that of a circle around a centre—and the form is symbolic of our life. The centre is the focus of our public life; meetings are held there, committees sit, problems are discussed, solutions found. One special committee sat long in continuous, earnest session to work out the new form of Jewish village life; in this difficult, intensive work the woman had no part.

At that time all the families lived in wooden barracks of uniform pattern. Between barracks, a space of twenty meters; in each barrack a family—husband, wife, little tots. This was the hardest time in our life. The men worked together; they ploughed the fields in common, for these were not yet divided out. In common they also did the magnificent job of draining all the swamps in the Nahalal region.

Not a cow had yet been bought. Gardens were without hedges and without water. The produce was divided among families on a per capita basis, and there was barely enough to keep life going. Oil and kerosene were measured almost with a dropper. Collecting her day's supplies, feeding the children, gathering branches for fuel, cooking, washing the children and putting them to sleep, stopping up the holes and cracks in the walls—this took every instant of a woman's time.

And, later, lying in bed, I used to think: "Tomorrow—the same round." One thought tormented me: "What power compels me to stand such close, daily guard over my petty private interests?" What cord bound me, and could that cord never be broken?

That time did not last long: but it sticks in the memory like an intolerable day of hot desert wind in the Jordan Valley.

The first productive work given women in Nahalal was tending geese. Why geese, of all things, I don't remember; but I do remember that we all went at it with vast enthusiasm. At that, we did not have much joy of our work; I least of all. Geese are too libertarian; they like freedom, disorder and company. It was a regular, troublesome job, every evening, to gather one's geese, separate them out from one's neighbor's, and drive them home. But at other times, when I stepped into the night, and I saw those white patches on the dark field, and heard the quack-quack of their conversations, it seem to me that this was the authentic voice of the young colony, and then a happy warmth poured through my heart.

That first period passed without satisfaction and without creativity; and then the first money came for the upbuilding of the settlement. We bought cows—but they were Arab cows, which are niggardly with their milk.

Still—they were cows. Their voices came to us from the stalls—and sometimes the milkpail would have something in it.

We began to plant orchards and vineyards, to keep chickens and turkeys, to plant and water vegetables. The place began to hum. Hands and heads were busy all day long; the work took everything, body and mind.

Then came the years of growth. The children grew; the numbers of the cattle grew; the coops became more crowded, the summits of the fruit trees reached higher, the stocks in the vineyard spread out their nets.

The great, free world of creative work opened its gates to the woman.

Nahalal   D. D.

THE WOMEN'S FARM IN NACHLATH
JEHUDAH

WE, THE *chalutzoth* (women pioneers) of the third immigration stream of 1919 to 1923, found it hard to understand the women workers' movement of Palestine. We had
been brought up in and by the Russian revolution, at a
time when women were occupying important economic and
cultural positions. We believed that the wall which divided
man's work from woman's had fallen forever. I, at least,
was therefore astonished to find in Palestine separate
women workers' institutions. If the enterprises to be found
in the women workers' farms are also to be found in the
general farms, why the separate farms? But before long
the realities of Palestinian life taught me to approach the
woman question in quite another way.

Soon after my arrival I went to work in one of the *kvutzoth* in Galilee. I was bitterly disappointed when I perceived how small the role was which the women played,
how weak their influence on the common system. And
doubt awoke in me. It was possible that the woman comrade
did not earn her own keep, brought in less than she used
up! Would it therefore not be better for me to return to my
earlier work, and be a teacher again? There at least I
would be sure of doing creative work, and of feeling no
difference between myself and the men comrades. I was
offered the post of teacher in a large *kvutzah* which had a
school; I promised to give my answer shortly, and meanwhile set out for the town of Tel Aviv.

On the way I made a detour to the farm of women
workers at Nachlath Jehudah. The work of the women
there made a tremendous impression on me. Here were

women carrying on without help, on their own initiative and responsibility, and doing as well as the men. I made up my mind to try once more for land work. Hannah Chisick, who directed the place, proposed that I work half-days on the farm, and in the evenings teach the women Hebrew. I accepted.

We worked under difficult conditions. The farm got its water from the colony of Nachlath Jehudah. We had no cistern or pipes of our own. I and another woman were busy all day long lugging cans of water from the barrels while another comrade had to run every so often to the colony council to plead for more water. And as soon as there was a quarrel between ourselves and the council, they threatened to cut off the water. And there were actually days when we had to bring our water from Rishon le-Zion, if we did not want the shoots in the nursery to wither and die, or let the cattle and fowl go thirsty. The summer was embittered by this situation and only in the rainy winter season did we breathe freely.

But in spite of all the hardships and suffering the work had life and content. The colonists who came to see "the work of the girl pioneers" had nothing but praise. It was a joy to look at the tree nursery. Before long our settlement had made a name for itself as a model farm. The women believed in themselves and in the path they were indicating for the women workers of Palestine.

I worked, as a matter of fact, all day long, and evenings I taught the girls. Teaching was a sort of continuation of the day's occupation; the lessons in Hebrew and in working class literature were echoes of our daily experience.

In the winter we sold the nursery, and the colony balance-sheet showed a profit. This was triumph! It showed that the women workers' farm could stand on its own feet.

The settlement lacked not only water, but land. The National Fund had given us twenty-five dunams (about six acres) —but there was a neighboring plot of sixty dunams which the National Fund was supposed to buy for us. In the meantime, however, we used to rent land either from Arabs or from the Jewish colonists of Rishon le-Zion. The story of how we bought the additional land for the women's farm of Nachlath Jehudah is long and complicated, but it is probably without a parallel in the history of the workers' movement in Palestine.

I shall give it in brief. Ever since this settlement was founded, in 1922, negotiations had been going on for that extra patch of sixty dunams. In the meantime the economic condition of the colony of Nachlath Jehudah went from bad to worse. The consequence was much quarreling between the colonists, and a perpetual bitterness of which we were frequently the victims.

When we saw that the perpetual threat of cutting off the water supply was endangering our tree nursery, which was the hub of our economy, we sent two women to the central office of the land workers' organization in Jerusalem, and to the Zionist Executive. We demanded a cistern for ourselves. This time we got it. As a rule we would fill the cistern in the evening, when the colony was not drawing water, and the supply would last us two or three days. It made things easier.

That had nothing to do, of course, with the fundamental problem of more land. Negotiations continued—and the owners suddenly doubled their price. The National Fund refused to pay the new high price; and we almost talked our hearts out, almost wore ourselves to nothing, before we managed to bring about an agreement. But it was bought in the end, and we looked forward with longing for the summer when the deep plough would pass over the land, and the new land would be added in part to the vegetable garden and in part to the nursery. We also planned to have a vineyard and a patch to be sown with grass for the fowl and the cattle.

How easy it was to work after the new land was bought—it was as if we had become winged beings. We did not feel at all that we were working here temporarily, that the day would come when we would have to pack up, and find, each one for herself, a permanent place. The work was the main thing, and aside from it nothing mattered, neither our past nor our future. But I was aware of an obscure fear that on the general farms I would be swallowed up again by the powerful traditions of our feminine past, and I would no longer know the joy of independent, self-supporting work.

And now the big moment approached. We were expecting the tractor which was to do the deep ploughing, when suddenly there was a change of heart in the colony. A few men called the others together and persuaded them to prevent the ploughing. They too were in need of land. No one was worrying about *their* plight, and so in protest they would prevent *us* from ploughing our new land until land was bought for them too! The tractor came. The colonists stood by their resolution, and no ploughing was done. We tried to argue with them, we threatened and pleaded—in vain. The tractor stood idle for a few days, and finally returned. A profound depression settled on our farm—all our hopes were dashed to the ground.

And only a year later did we see the land ploughed. Part of it was turned over to the colonists and part of it to us. We began at last to carry out the complete plans of the settlement.

Ain Charod   MIRIAM SCHLIMOWITCH.

THE TOBACCO *KVUTZAH*

WHEN our little *kvutzah* or commune of women building-trade workers had finished putting up the house of comrade M. it found itself confronted by the major problem of "to be, or not to be." We were holding the last position which women had won for themselves in the building trade; and it was hard to give this up. But employment at building was getting scarcer and scarcer, while within our hearts the longing for agriculture was growing stronger and stronger. In the end we were approached with a plan to transform ourselves into a women workers' *kvutzah* for tobacco. The place was to be K'far Tabor (Meschah). We accepted the offer of the Agricultural Office of the Labor Federation and were sent to K'far Tabor. We had, by that time, become scattered throughout the country; and it was no easy job getting us together again. But finally we arrived, some on foot, others in carts, at our new home. This was toward the end of 1923.

The plan of the Agricultural Office was to create a women's working and training *kvutzah* on the plan of the farms for women workers already existing in Judæa: vegetables, dairy farming and chicken raising. The difference would be that, instead of occupying ourselves with tree culture we would work on tobacco. There were to be twenty women in the group. The planting of the nursery for the tobacco shoots was to begin only in the spring. In the meantime the colonists would employ us at tobacco packing. This was the agreement between the Agricultural Office and the Union of Galilee Colonists. Also we were to live in a big wooden barrack. The barrack, we were told before setting out, was already on the spot. We would only have to put it up. Land had been rented for us from the colonists. We were to be initiated into the tobacco work by an expert. Other details would become clear in time.

The beginning of the enterprise did not augur very well. On arriving we found that employment at binding tobacco was very hard to get. Even those workers who had long been on the spot could not find jobs. The barrack "already on the spot" was a myth. The rains began and we had not yet found a suitable piece of ground for our settlement; the actual plot which had been rented lay at a considerable distance from the colony, and within the colony there were no empty plots. It began to look as though the whole idea was absolutely chimerical. We only wondered what on earth we had been sent up here for. . . .

Then the comrades came up from the Agricultural Office. They got down to details, in regard to work and the budget. Money was appropriated for cows and chickens; a certain sum was fixed for each one of us to keep us going — a pound and a half a month. The total budget, an advance on our tobacco earnings, consisted of fifty pounds for the barrack and twelve pounds per comrade, the latter provided by the Zionist Executive.

This was the plan. Unfortunately it just did not work out.

We were supposed to earn our keep during the winter at tobacco packing, but it soon became clear that only a few of us would find work there. We therefore began to look for work elsewhere, and this naturally brought us into conflict with the other workers, who had been here before our coming and were now out of jobs. We were looked upon, by these workers, as spoiled and pampered persons; the Agricultural Office and the Zionist Executive were looking after us, while *they* depended on their daily earnings. The upshot of it all was that by the end of the winter our *kvutzah* had a big deficit.

Just before Passover four of our members went to Tiberias to bake *matzoth*. We thought that, with their pay, we would cover the winter loss. But this too turned out to be a dream—the pay was too low. And we couldn't get rid of the job for the simple reason that the responsibility for its execution had been assumed by the Labor Office in Tiberias. So our comrades had to work to the bitter end and come back empty-handed.

These were the "side-incomes" we earned! We were always compelled to do record jobs for the lowest pay. And meanwhile our own little farm began to clamor for our attention—just at the moment, naturally, when side-work was becoming more plentiful.

The greatest part of our time and energy was absorbed by the nursery for the tobacco. But it was worth while. It became the finest nursery in the colony. It ripened in time and gave us healthy shoots which took at once in the field. The colonists prophesied that we were going to become rich. "Experts" estimated that we had enough shoots to cover one hundred dunams of soil. But here too we were doomed to disappointment. We had barely enough for fifty. Instead of dropping the grain by handfuls, we planted it in rows, and two-thirds of the plot was wasted.

The winter garden gave us little joy at first—which is usual with gardens which are cultivated extensively on grain land. Besides, we were late. When the rains began we had not yet got our seed for cabbages and cauliflower; the few beds of carrots and radishes were not successful, and when the potatoes became ripe they were systematically stolen.

We lost considerably on that garden. Not only did we fail to pay back the cost of the ploughing (I am leaving our own work out of the account); we barely got enough of an income to cover the seed and the fertiliser.

But for all that the work in the garden was good. At the worst times the beets and tomatoes helped us out a little. Moreover, we were learning—and this meant a great deal for the women who had never worked on the land before.

The barrack was a continual pest. We planned to bring

it over before the rains began—and put it up when the rains were on and there was plenty of free time. The exact opposite happened. The barrack was bought in the nearby Arab town of Jenin—but not before mid-winter. To bring it to K'far Tabor through the mud and rain would have cost too much; so we got it in the early spring when there was plenty of work to do among the colonists. We just about managed to put the barrack up on the public place in the colony before the time for tobacco planting came. The women themselves laid the foundations and did all the inside construction work. From the wood that was left over we managed to put up two more buildings: a coop for the chickens which had hatched, and a stall for the cows. In fact our *kvutzah*, which had originally belonged to the building trade, managed somehow to exercise its old craft till the last day of our stay in K'far Tabor.

We were more fortunate with our hens. Looking after chickens does *not* come under the heading of "light work" —especially when the chickens are being kept as "lodgers" in someone else's yard. But our chickens responded magnificently. Ten hens gave us seventy chicks. We did not eat many of the eggs. At first we left them to be hatched, and later we fed them to the chicks. After that the hens stopped laying. But if not for the few eggs we did get, and if not for the young chicks, God knows what would have happened to many of our members, who, during that summer, went almost into a conspiracy of sickness.

The buying of the cows for our colony was handed over to one of the expert colonists. He did not trust the local product, and made a journey, therefore, to Golan in Transjordania among the Bedouins, and came back with two cows and two calves, magnificent animals, wild and healthy as the land they were born in. One of the cows had a massive head almost like an ox, and the mere sight of her was terrifying.

The cows were brought before the barrack was ready, they, too, were therefore "lodged out." They were difficult animals to handle, and it was not always possible to milk them. It took us a month to break them in. Then the pasture gave out and the maize was not yet ready; other food was hard to get. And when the girl who looked after the cows fell sick, and another girl began to milk them, they seemed to fall to pieces. They stopped giving milk and turned so wild again that it was dangerous to go near them.

It almost came to a catastrophe. One day the girl went to milk the cows, and found herself caught between the two animals, and could not extricate herself from the narrow stall. The animals went wild, and began to take revenge on her for their sufferings. After this incident we had no alternative but to sell the wilder of the two animals, with its calf, to the colonist who had brought them. The other cow, which we also stopped milking shortly after, stood there in the yard like a fifth wheel on a cart. Unfortunately this "wheel" had to be fed, and not until at the end of the year did we get rid of it.

When the *kvutzah* was ultimately dissolved, and each of us went her own way, the last darling calf, to which we had given the affectionate name of *Chaim-Yankel,* also went his way—to wit, on the long journey from which no Palestinian or any other calf ever returns.

But to resume the story. The tobacco, as I have said, was our principal occupation, and was supposed to make good all the losses we had incurred elsewhere.

We worked hard at the picking of the leaves, staying in the fields from dawn to evening. Our food was poor. We went out without having had even a cup of tea, and only at ten o'clock—almost after a day's work—did we get our first bite. Our strength began to give way. The numbers that went out every morning decreased, and with them decreased, naturally enough, the work turned out.

At the end of the summer we fell victims to a new epidemic, "weakness." The women crawled rather than walked around, with low temperatures, their legs giving way under them, their heads always aching. It was impossible to send these women to the hospital, and the doctor's advice sounded like a poor joke: "Plenty of good food, eggs, milk, etc. . . ."

The bad food prevented us from getting better. By the month of Elul (September) we had no one fit to work in the kitchen. As soon as a girl tried, she collapsed. Our barrack looked like a hospital.

When we first came to K'far Tabor we were quite certain of success; we were going to make money. And the shopkeepers and colonists must have felt the same way, because they gave us all the credit we wanted. A few months later the pressure of the debts began to make itself felt. We begrudged ourselves even our meagre meals, and every extra penny had to go to the shopkeepers. Whenever we got an order on the cooperative supply of the Galilee colonists, part of it was deducted on account of the debts. And when our *kvutzah* began to buy direct in Tiberias, we had to pay out part of our purchases. On top of our general distress we had the uncomfortable feeling that our creditors were in the right.

The little debts tormented us more than the big ones. There were certain things that we simply could not do without: milk for the sick, wheat, straw for the animals, cotton thread, etc.—and all this we could not get for cash; we had to have credit. There were two sources of loss—in the buying and in the selling. We became experts in exchanging goods; some of the women were so skilled that without them our whole machinery would have stopped working. And the time, the energy, the labor we expended on all this! It seems to me that only for the sake of a *kvutzah* would people put up with this sort of thing. But that daily struggle with pettinesses degraded the ideal which had brought us all to the village.

So far I have said nothing about the extraordinary qualities which became evident among the members of our group during those hard times. The responsibility was car-

ried by all of us, and we were bound together by our love
of the work, and during the darkest days this love was our
one reservoir of strength, our one consoling possession.
We looked upon the belongings of the *kvutzah* as something sacred, and guarded the common store from the
smallest loss. The women were considerate of each other
in the division of the work. Above all, no complaints were
heard even in the most difficult hours. When new comrades came up they were inducted into the work and in a
short time they were on the same footing as the old.

But we had gone off the beaten track into a place where
the labor element was lacking, and a cultural life was impossible. Those women who could have helped us in this
respect were too taken up with their physical tasks. We
hadn't the money for books, or even for a subscription to
a newspaper; and the continuous, draining labor, together
with the unprescribed hours, prevented us from concentrating on cultural work. Once or twice we exerted ourselves and started something, but we had to let it fall.

It was only when the final decision came to dissolve the
kvutzah that we flung ourselves on books. A few of our
girls began to read the works of A. D. Gordon; we knew
that our sufferings had not yet come to an end—but we
wanted at least to understand what we were suffering for.

Deganiah Beth   Tovah Jaffa.

THE BIRTH OF THE CHAVURAH

THE big crisis began in Palestine in the year 1925, and its first and hardest blows fell on the women workers. In the labor councils of the towns it was not understood that special methods must be applied to the problem of the women in the crisis, and even the most thoughtful leaders seemed to believe that there was no way of combating women's unemployment.

A mood of despair seized the women workers in the cities. All ways seemed to be closed. There were new girl pioneers who had been preparing for years before they entered the country, loyal and steadfast spirits; and even they began to fall under the influence of the enemies of the Federation of Labor and of the working class. The small group of communists exploited, at all town meetings, this mood of despair, and a feeling of resentment began to rise against the Federation of Labor which was accused of "sacrificing the women workers."

The few training farms of women workers which then existed could absorb a few dozen more women; and the handful of women who entered the communes of mixed workers remained idle. When the men workers began to feel the crisis, the women had already been suffering for some time. The Women Workers' Council tried to introduce women into the building trade, but without real success. One by one the women left the new trade, and only a few obstinate spirits remained. The situation became steadily worse. The Women's Committee in the Executive of the Federation looked in vain for a solution.

It was then—in the winter of 1926—that Hannah Chisick suggested the formation of the *chavurah* form of commune in the towns and in the colonies. In the *meshek* women work on a communal basis while they learn agriculture; agriculture is, however, their main occupation and purpose. In the *chavurah* there would be some agriculture too, but the main support would be the wages earned by members at outside employment, in factories or in farms. The capacity of the *meshek* was limited to the needs of the settlement and its economy. But the *chavurah* could always expand. In the *chavurah* the land work would be intensive—an inner support; outside work would be taken wherever it could be found. Evenings the outside worker would return to the *chavurah*. She would have a home. The organisation would help her to fight her battles, and would relieve her, too, of the dreadful loneliness of her own life. The purpose of the *chavurah* was therefore manifold, and it aimed at nothing less than the transformation of the life of the individual woman worker, and its integration with a collective life in new surroundings. The inner, agricultural work of the *chavurah*, beside supporting the institution, would also give it a character of permanence, binding the comrades to the place and to each other.

This new proposal was placed before the Central Women Workers' Committee, and it was so timely that it was accepted at once. On its side, the Labor Department of the Zionist Executive set aside a certain sum for the founding of the *chavuroth*.

During the crisis most of the men workers, and a great many of the women, received the famous *siyuah*—the dole —but the women workers' movement conquered its own despair and broke for itself the demoralising influence of this reluctantly accepted form of help. Hundreds of workless women preferred to join the *chavuroth*, and most of the members of the Women Workers' Council occupied themselves with the direction of this new form of labor collective. It should be mentioned that at this time another effort was made to relieve the distress of the women workers. Thanks to the efforts of the labor council of Tel Aviv large numbers of women were admitted to the factories.

The first *chavuroth* to be organized were those of Tel Aviv—one in the centre of the town, the other to the north. They took in sixty members. It may be said without exaggeration that today these two *chavuroth* are the finest institutions which the labor movement of Tel Aviv can boast. They created, in a short space of time, a model farm, and began to exert a profound influence—by their mere existence—on the women workers of the city.

In the spring of 1926 was held the third conference of the women workers, which accepted formally the plan of the *chavuroth*. The council proposed to the Zionist Executive that *chavuroth* be founded in different parts of the country; and so ready was the time for this work that, even before the Zionist Executive had accepted the plan, *chavuroth* began to spring up of their own accord. The Council was unable to concentrate and guide the creative energies which the proposal had released. Nor did the budget of the Council anywhere near meet the needs of the new institutions—the less so since part of the budget had to be spent directly on the unemployed.

But fortune was with the *chavuroth*. At the critical moment the newly founded Pioneer Women's Organisation in America forwarded the sums needed for the organisation of the new units.

The new *chavuroth* opened to the women workers doors which had been firmly closed to them till then. They began to play a significant role in the life of the Federation of Labor and created a new cultural element in the worker movement. Dozens of women got in the *chavurah* their first knowledge of land-work, and later spread this knowledge throughout the country.

Ain Charod   M. Sh.

THE CHAVURAH OF PETACH TIKVAH

WHEN, in the month of Elul (September) in 1926, a group of us decided to found a *chavurah* in Petach Tikvah, we had not received any promise of help. We simply went at it. From one of the *kvutzoth* we managed to get three old tents, and we set them up on the narrow lot opposite the Workers' Club in Petach Tikvah—much to the astonishment of the passers-by.

The morning after we had set up the tents, we went out to look for work. Meanwhile a grocer promised us food on credit until the first wages came in. We were five in number at the outset, and two weeks later our number had swelled by an additional seven, all new arrivals in Palestine. They came to our *chavurah* because they were out of work; they had heard about us, but what a *chavurah* was, and what life in general meant in Palestine, they scarcely understood. Only yesterday these youngsters had left their parents' homes in Europe; their bodies had not yet been broken in to physical work. And evenings we all sat in the tents silent, depressed, our minds filled with memories of home.

Winter was approaching, and the doubts grew with the nights: Would we succeed? Would we hold together and found a permanent *chavurah*? Would these new comrades stand up under the strain? Would we ultimately get a piece of land of our own, like the other *kvutzoth* in the colony? And would we be able to build a barrack before the rains came upon us?

What we longed for most was a piece of land of our own, so that we might create a little farm for ourselves. We knew, of course, that we were a *chavurah*, and not a *meshek*; farming and land-work would therefore never be our main occupation; but all of us felt the same desire to see the first green things starting up on *our* patch of soil. After much effort the Agricultural Office of the Federation of Labor obtained a piece of land for us in the colony, and we moved to our new quarters. New comrades came to us every day, and we had to put up a new tent. And then the winter came.

We were afraid of the first rain; the tents stood on an elevation and were not protected from the wind. And then the clouds opened suddenly, and a shout of laughter and happiness went through the tents. Every new burst of rain evoked in those young hearts a new burst of joy. On the morning after the first rain we broke the ground for our vegetable garden.

The struggle for work was long and cruel. The majority of the women, whether individual or belonging to the mixed communes, were content with minor jobs, the kind of thing that was considered suitable for women. The *chavurah* was the first institution in the colony to drop the distinction, and to demand work of any kind. The only measure was the physical strength of the worker. Our example was followed by the other women in the colony. Our group soon became famous among the colonists.

Evenings the girls came home from the work which it had been so difficult to find. The table was narrow, the food meagre, but the conversation eager and comradely. There were always new things to tell. And after supper we went off to the colony to a meeting or a lecture. Frequently enough there were reports read in our own group. Our folk had worked themselves into the life of the colony; and if they were absent from some occasion, it was noticed at once.

The barrack for the kitchen and dining-room was not finished until well on in the rainy season. We had no incubator of our own, and we did not wish to lose a whole year; so for the first period we brought forth our chicks in the *chavurah* in north Tel Aviv. And when we had the chicks we crowded a little closer together and made room for them in a section of the barracks. We still slept in tents, of course. After the chicks we brought in beehives.

Winter was raging now. Every day another tent would go over in the wind—and every day new girls came to join the *chavurah*. The *chavurah* grew steadily, and the new comrades, as they came along, absorbed its spirit readily and threw themselves heartily into the work.

Our little daily worries and triumphs made the time pass quickly; here was the winter gone, and we were still in tents. The whole institution—chickens, nursery, beehives— had grown and thriven. The "new" comrades had become part of our life, and felt themselves bound to the world of the worker and its ideals. The first year passed and we could say with a calm certainty that we had been successful; we had founded a new economic unit of workers.

Chavurah of Petach Tikvah. REBECCA BROISMAN.

WOMEN BUILD HOUSES

THE town of Tel Aviv was in the full swing of expansion. For the first time thousands of Jews had entered the building trade and had mastered it. And the Jewish woman worker began to batter at the doors of the trade. But it was not so easy to get in.

The men had quite a number of reasons for keeping us out. Some said the work was too strenuous for women. Others argued that if women were admitted into the building trade communes, which contracted for work as a group, the output would decrease and the pay with it. The women were not very sure of themselves—but they pressed hard for admission. The fight went on for quite a time, and finally the workers' council of Tel Aviv decided that every building trade *kvutzah* had to admit two women.

This was the way I was admitted to one of the *kvutzoth*. I knew that I was being received not spontaneously, but under orders. The whole struggle semed to me a fantastic thing. I asked myself: Have the men forgotten the time— it was only yesterday—when they too were unskilled, and their contracts resulted in deficits? And aren't there, among men too, the strong and the weak, the efficient and the inefficient. Why this hostile attitude, from the outset, to the woman worker?

I remembered, too, that before setting out for Palestine I had worked everywhere in the *Chalutz* organisation—the preparatory schools for pioneers in Europe—on a footing of absolute equality with the men. In time, I used to think, we will establish the same equality in Palestine. But when I got here I could not stand the amused irony, the patronising, superior attitude of the stronger toward the weaker. I wanted, therefore, to give up my right to enter the build-

ing *kvutzah;* but friends of mine in the **Women Workers'**
Council persuaded me to hold on; just because the men
looked at it as they did, it was my duty to go in, and to try
and create a new relationship.

Without any particular liking for it, I reported to the
tent which housed the Council of the *kvutzah.* The place
was jammed with noisy, arguing men, and the moment I
entered I was aware of a reaction of astonishment. One of
the men made a silly joke about "our suffragettes," but the
man in charge turned out to be friendly. He told me what
kind of work I was to do, and when I would start. I went
out of the tent encouraged.

I knew that the first days would be the hardest. In every
group of men you are sure to find some who like to make
a newcomer the butt of their jokes—and woe to the new-
comer if he doesn't know how to take it. I also knew that
there was a great difference between the land-work in the
Chalutz organisation, or the "black labor" (our Palestinian
name for heavy, unskilled work) which I had been doing
till now, and the cement work which I would begin tomorrow.

At five o'clock I reported. The leader of the group
showed every one his place; mine was with the cement
workers.

A couple of workers rolled up a barrel of cement, and
emptied it on a heap of sand and stones. I stood by and
poured on water while the men mixed. The mixture, when
ready, was carried over to the building place in buckets or
on planks.

They worked slowly at first, yesterday's weariness still
being in their limbs. Gradually the work livened up. Gradually I too was caught up in the rhythm of it. One of the
men began to sing, the others joined in, all in time with
the work. Everything became light and easy and joyous.

But in comparison with the tasks of the men, mine was

a trifling one, and I felt the slight. "Is this going to be my day's work?" I asked.

One of the men answered my question with another: "What other kind of work can we give a woman?"

"Well, who used to pour the water before I came?"

"We used to take turns."

I said I would take turns too. I was not going to pour water all day long.

So I changed off with one of the men, and began to carry cement. The comrade who loaded the cement on to the plank said: "That's all right. Let her lift this a couple of times—she'll be asking for something easier."

And I must confess that the load nearly made me stagger. But I called up all my will-power, and walked with steady steps, as if this was the most usual thing for me. I knew a dozen pair of eyes were watching me slyly, and if I faltered once there would be a shout of laughter.

Later I noticed that the comrade who did the loading was putting more on my plank than on anyone else's. I understood—and said nothing. After a while I stood still, and looked at him with a smile. He became confused. The comrade who carried the plank with me kept complaining that it was too heavy. He wondered how on earth I could lift my end, and became angry with the loader. But I asked him to keep quiet and wait. I was right. The next time the load was considerably lighter, and the loader got his share of abuse from the others.

The same story was repeated when it came to filling in the foundations. And in this way a fight went on between me and a couple of the men, all day long, until I forced them to give way. The next day they confessed that instead of getting a laugh at my expense, they had learned to respect me.

My reputation as a good worker was soon established, and I was looked upon as one of the best. When the elections came round for the council of the building workers, my name was put up.

There isn't very much to this story. I only tell it to help make clear the struggle which the women workers of Palestine had to wage when trying to break into a new field.

TECHIAH.

THE "INDEPENDENT" WOMAN

THE working woman has one ideal: she wants to work
and earn on a footing of equality with her husband. And in
order to do this she has to employ a girl to look after the
house. And at once a "class-contrast" is created, and little
conflicts become unavoidable. I come home evenings after
a heavy day's work, and I find the house not done. It ang-
ers me. Isn't it the duty of the girl to keep the house clean
and in order? But this girl is a comrade of mine, and she
surely didn't come to Palestine for the purpose of dusting
the rooms in my house. She surely left her home over there
after a bitter struggle with her parents because she couldn't
stand the old family life and the old family work; now she
is trapped in the same round, and with strangers!

But what about me, her "employer"? When I get home
after a full day's work, another day's work begins for me,
because in her eight working hours she can't get through.
So when I do get a free moment I can't keep my eyes open.
What, then, has happened with our struggle for a fixed
working-day?

And for us women of the towns I see only two alterna-
tives, and both of them lead us away from our goal. The
first is to leave our trades and become old-fashioned housewives once more, supported by our husbands; the second is
to be both worker and housewife. . . .

And a new question comes up. We, the women workers
of Palestine, regard our work as something primary in our
lives; through work we will regain our personalities. And
yet I must ask myself, what is my authentic inner relationship to my work? Why did I feel so utterly wretched when
my husband was unemployed? Would I have felt so bad
about it if *he* had been working, and *I* had been unem-

ployed? I am compelled to answer, No! The despair of the
woman when her husband is not earning is grounded in
something more than mere economics, for that attitude is
unchanged even if she is earning enough to keep the entire
household going.

It may be that this curious attitude toward our own
work has to do with the instinctive knowledge that some
day we will have to leave the work because of the child.
And therefore—though we do not acknowledge it—we
have a different, a lighter relationship to our own work.
And this relationship deprives us of what is most important in life—belief in our own forces, respect for our own
selves. And we will never know the feeling of harmonious
work as long as we do not know a complete inner compulsion to earn our own livelihood.

And when we do find a woman who has complete faith
in her own strength, we see her crumbling under the double
yoke—her job and her family.

And of course we rebel against the intolerable yoke
which such a woman carries. And is nothing left but that
my comrade, whom I take into the house, shall assume the
burden of the family which I myself am not willing to bear?

Tel Aviv. HANNAH.

"COMRADE SO-AND-SO'S WIFE"

IN PALESTINE there came a parting of the ways. Over there, in the Russian exile, men and women had been equal comrades in the movement. We worked together, suffered together in the prisons and in the remote countries to which we were expelled; the moment the first pioneer certificates reached us, admitting us into Palestine, we were divided into the two classes: men comrades and women comrades.

The very first instructions we got from Palestine hinted at this inequality, and when we landed we were actually separated into two groups. In the one group were those who were "building the country"; in the other were those who would take care, in every-day matters, of "the builders of the country." And always we hear the same formula: "This piece of work will need so many men, and the men will employ so many women. . . ."

Over there, in the exile, we had passed through a common preparation, in the schools and in the movement. *Here* the women workers have organised themselves into a separate labor movement. In the exile we felt ourselves to be adult participants in the social process; here our education begins again in the kindergarten.

We found here hardly any bond or relationship between the unmarried working girl, who feels that she is a full-fledged member of the Federation of Labor, and the working woman who is married. It was not a change of status in the life of the same women—it was a division into two worlds. And this explains the unnaturalness of the women worker's movement and the inner struggles and contradictions in the soul of the women comrades.

When a man comrade chooses a trade, he enters into a permanent relationship with his professional union. But

the woman feels within herself—and others are there to
remind her—that she is only a guest, a temporary member,
in the trade organisation. And when she marries she has
not even the right to the professional status of "house-
worker"—no, not though she meets completely the statu-
tory demand of the Federation of Labor, which says that
those are entitled to membership who live solely by their
own physical or mental labor, without employing someone
else. No, she is admitted into the Federation as "comrade
So-and-so's wife."

It is true that the housewife has the legal right to her
own membership card in the Federation; but as the dues are
obligatory only in the case of the bread-winners of the
family, few women have availed themselves of their privilege, and they remain on the roll as "wives of comrades."

And perhaps that invidious title "wife of comrade So-
and-so" does belong properly to such women as come into
the labor movement only through their husbands: but does
it fit those women who were brought up in the Palestine
labor movement, and who did their duty by it for many
years?

And who of us has not seen "comrade So-and-so's wife"
working in other people's houses, or doing other people's
laundry, while her children run around neglected, or cared
for by her out-of-work husband? Who has not seen those
unhappy women who, without any help from the Federation of Labor, carry the full burden of their little children
and of a chronically sick husband? Are not these women
entitled to a place in the Federation as full-fledged members, and not merely as the wives of comrades?

This transition from "member" to "member's wife" in-
fluences the whole of our social life. Even at the Women
Workers' Conferences the married members occupy a separate rubric—"Workers' Wives."

We forget too often that the "wife of comrade So-and-
so" is a mother who must bring up a new generation in the
tradition of the Federation of Labor. The women workers'

movement has sinned against labor in not having provided such women with a special role, special duties and functions. Had this not happened we would not now be faced by the fact that not only is the woman a "temporary" member of the Federation, but actually a temporary member in the labor movement! We should not have to be witnesses of a situation in which the home of the comrade is gradually weaned away, in spirit, from the ideals of the Labor Federation.

The "member's wife" has little share in social life; she is seldom to be found even at those gatherings which are occupied with her personal problems, such as parents' meetings in the schools, in the trade organisation to which her husband belongs, at the conferences of the workers' quarters in which her family is inscribed—not even though, later on, she will have to obey all the resolutions which are passed there. The workingclass mother is so sunk in her daily work and worries, and so exhausted by them, that she becomes separated from her own class, and is wholly isolated from the world.

And is there no way out of the *impasse?* In the individualist cooperative settlement (the *moshav ovdim*) there is a system of mutual help among the women not less than among the men. And though it is true that the labor class is more scattered in the towns, and is likewise less strongly unified, it is not impossible to institute a system of mutual help. We need good children's homes, communal kitchens, playgrounds which should be open several hours a day, and on Saturdays and holidays as well. We also need a separate sick fund, so that we can substitute for the sick mother in the house and in looking after the children. As things are now the sick housewife must either go on working until she collapses and her children are simply thrown on the street, or else she must get "cheap" help. All this could be avoided if the bond between the workingclass mother and her kind were not allowed to break, if the women workers' movement would not treat us like an alienated branch of the organisation—if, in brief, *our* problem were considered everyone's problem.

The path which lies before the workingclass mother is not an easy one, nor has it yet been marked out. It is one which uses up the person, leaving scars forever on the soul; and much of this suffering is due to the unjust attitude adopted toward us by the group.

Tel Aviv   ZIPPORAH BAR-DROMA.

SARAH CHISICK
From Her Letters and Diaries

Milchamiah, Adar, 1915—from a diary

On the fifth of Adar we got up very early—my father, two brothers, a sister and myself—and packed food for the whole day. We got into the cart of a colonist who was going to Deganiah, past our field. A quarter of an hour beyond the colony, the Jordan showed itself, transparent and still. But that stillness was only on the surface, because the heart of the Jordan is an angry one. We began to pass across, struggling with the swift waters, which tore at the sides of the cart and forced their way in.

Our field is a broad meadow on the east bank of the Jordan. We begin to uproot the weeds. Around us—peace and silence. Now and again we hear the croaking of a frog, or the sudden trill of birds.

We are alone here, alone in a sea of waving wheat. Most of the fields are Arab, a few of them Jewish. When we stand up straight and look toward the east, we see the lovely, broad meadows stretching far away to the foot of the Transjordan hills; and our hearts beat faster when we think—each one of us to himself—how many Jewish colonies could be planted on this empty space! And when we turn round and look westward all the colonies look back at us—especially our own Milchamiah, with its roofs and green orchards twinkling in the sunlight. There among the hills, westward from the Sea of Galilee, shines Puriah, which rich Americans have bought lately; and on the southern shore of Galilee is Deganiah, which belongs to the Jewish National Fund. And somewhat to the west, on the same shore, you see the colony Kinereth.

Ekron, 29th of Shebet, 1919—from a letter to a friend

It is eight o'clock in the evening, and I am sitting in the house. Some of the girls have gone to bed, others are reading in their rooms. Our house is a small one, and stands outside the colony. In front it is guarded by eucalyptus trees, and behind is a little flower garden. A true village house, especially from the outside.

Rebeccah! You write me that what I need is a place where one can live as well as work. But I already feel myself bound to the fields and to land work, and I cannot do without them. Now, having learned a little about the town, I have begun to appreciate the work in the village! But it is very doubtful whether I will ever find a place where everything will satisfy me. I only let myself dream that there will be a *kvutzah* where I—or rather we, you and Chayah and myself—will work together. If it would only come true!

I feel well. All day long your sister Judith and I dug beet-roots and radishes. That's easy and pleasant work. We are proud of our beet-roots (I can say *our* beet-roots, can't I?); the beans are blossoming, the peas and onions are coming out beautifully. We are sowing summer vegetables and have planted tomatoes. The landscape round Ekron is lovely. To the south the horizon lies far, far away, level; to the south are the hills of Judæa, which have a habit of changing distances. This Saturday we will have an outing among the hills.

. . .

Ekron, 27th Shebet, 1919—to a friend

My darling little Chazah! I am always dreaming that a time will come when you and I and other friends will work and live in one group. I know that we will easily fit together. How happy we shall be, and how well the work will be divided. It is going to be a big enterprise, with many branches. And Chayah! I am sure that we won't keep accounts with each other about the work; our lives will be an

example of equality. We shall give much to our work, and
we shall take much from it. . . .

.   .   .

From the diary—1919

I am twenty-one years old! That means that I have lived
twenty-one years. How easily that is said! No, I have not
lived all these years—for a long time I only breathed.

I was once very naive—perhaps I still am. I used to be
beside myself when I saw all the bad things that are done
in the world. Why is it that good and honest people have
not the power over wicked people? And what hurts and an-
gers me most is that the wicked are always proclaimed as
the good and honest, while the really honest must suffer in
silence. I am not speaking just so; I have seen these things
in actual life. And more than once I have felt that all is
vanity, and life is loathsome.

One hope and only one is left me. What if that should
also be extinguished?

It is the hope to be a daughter of my people which is
rejecting the life it has known till now in order to become
a people of labor in its own home on its own soil.

I want to believe that this time, in spite of everything,
right will triumph; I want to see the triumph and rejoice in
it myself. . . .

.   .   .

From the diary—1919

I have heard the "good" news—the pogroms in Poland
and in the Ukraine. My heart aches for my brothers and
sisters; but more for my sisters, because their death is double. They die for being Jewish and for being women. God!
What bestiality! What lowness and vileness!

I often say to myself that I do not yet know life. But I
do know what human beings are; they are something un-
worthy of their name.

.   .   .

K'far Gileadi, Iyar 1919—*to a friend*
  Shalom, Rebeccah!

This is to tell you that we made the journey safely. I'll give you all the details.

Before we left Ayeleth ha-Shachar I felt bad—I don't know why. But as soon as we got on to the road, and we got the word, "Keep moving and keep quiet," I began to feel better. A little way out we met the others. They made a queer impression, sitting on the ground with their weapons in their hands and a sort of dreadful silence reigning over everything. They saw us and got up. We went on further. I took the revolver from K. and marched on firmly. I thought of that night in Petach Tikvah when the Turks came back unexpectedly, and all night long we went around silently and gave orders silently. But this time, as we went striding through the night, we felt a certain strength. After an hour's marching we came to a small lake. It was safe to talk now—and after the silence the men began to joke. Some wanted to walk through the lake as they were, shoes and everything. But we decided it would be best to take those off and wade through with naked feet. It did look queer, afterwards, thirty-five men sitting on the ground putting on their shoes again, in a silent night. . . . Now and again we heard the barking of a dog far away; and sometimes, in the distance, we caught the glimmer of the Huleh swamp.

At dawn we reached the slope of a hill, and after a rest began to climb. And as we went upward the slight of dawn increased. The scenery was glorious, especially Mount Hermon in the distance. All morning we climbed and crawled over hills and rocks, and at about one o'clock we got to K'far Gileadi. The most difficult part of the journey was coming down the abrupt slope. . . .

The surroundings here are beautiful. The group makes a good impression; the dangerous situation doesn't seem to affect them at all. Everyone is cheerful, and there is a good deal of singing.

PART IV

THE CHILD IN GROUP UPBRINGING

IV

THE CHILD IN GROUP UPBRINGING

FUNDAMENTAL PROBLEMS

I WANT to speak here about the group upbringing—as distinguished from the home upbringing — of children, about the place of this problem in our life, and about my work in it.

First: What impelled the *kvutzah* and the *kibutz*—the two forms of workers' communes—to abandon home for group upbringing?

The idea springs originally from the will to deepen the relationship and strengthen the bond between the individuals in the group. To this end we are ready to relinquish what is dearest to us into the hands of the collective whole. We know that the future of the group as such depends on the spirit in which our children are brought up. There is an additional motive: we want to make woman free in social and family life.

This group upbringing of children already has a history in Palestine, and a tradition has slowly been created. Unfortunately we are so absorbed and used up by the daily grind that we cannot go into the root principles of the question, though this would clarify many problems for us, and release new energies. At the present every *kvutzah* and *kibutz* has followed its own path; group upbringing is an established principle; but no general principle of method, and no general formulation of the problem, have yet been reached.

Is it possible, at this stage of our history, to sum up the results of this group upbringing, and state what it has given us? Can we say that the commune really feels itself to be the mistress of its own children? Have the parents been freed from the special worry of their own—and of nobody else's—children? And has the woman really been liberated?

It is not easy to answer the first two questions. From the outside it does look as though the children today belong to the *kvutzah*. In the actualities of life the thing has not gone so far by any means. The commune does try to see to it that its children shall lack nothing, either materially or spiritually. But what we consider of importance is the *inner* attitude of the group and of every individual comrade toward the children and the inner feeling of responsibility toward every new-born child.

The situation differs from *kvutzah* to *kvutzah*. The readiness to assume the cares of the upbringing of the children depends on the inner condition of the *kvutzah*, on the tone and spirit of the common life. And just as we have nowhere worked out fully a final and harmoniously interwoven living-together of the comrades, so we have not reached the final stage in which the children belong to the group as a whole.

And how is it with the parents? To us the act looks simple and natural enough; but it is not easy for the mother to relinquish her new-born child to the children's home.

There is much to be said about the general influence of the collective form of life on the family, but I want to consider only the fact that among us the child grows up away from the parents' home. In our form of life it is not easy, even in a general way, to create close and narrow bonds between parents and children. The hours of labor which we have to put in every day leave the father little time for his children, especially when the latter have a separate home, and have their own regulations. Sometimes the parents may be free but cannot visit the children because this would create disorder. In a family which lives its own separate life, it is the mother who creates the living relationship between father and child.

In our case, however, it is not the mother who feeds and tends the child, for the child enters into its own social life, and has its own group interests. Yet, in spite of this, our children always long for their parents and look forward eagerly to every meeting with them. The child suffers if the parents do not come when they are expected, and often the relationship between them is tense and nervous.

The real solution of the problem regarding the relation of the family to the communal group, and of the communal group to the child depends on two factors. First, will the collective be able to create that human atmosphere in which parents will give up their children to the group without fear or regret? Second, will the comrades who have no children of their own be prepared to share to the full the burden of the upbringing of the children, with its joy and suffering?

One thing we have achieved by our method of child upbringing, and that is the liberation of the mother in the group. For this we may be grateful. We see now that it is only by the method of group upbringing for the children that the mother can be a free member of the social structure. Once relieved of this heavy yoke, certain that everything will be done, physically and spiritually, for the good of her child, the mother can devote herself to the work which she has chosen. The very possibility of choosing her work gives the woman a footing of equality in the family and makes possible a free, unforced relationship between husband and wife.

In the whole complex of practical questions raised by our methods, the most important is this: does our children's home create for the young ones a separate and isolated little world, or is it part of the world of the grown-ups? In the small *kvutzah* this question is not altogether actual, for there the number of the children is small, and the whole place, with all its workings, is perpetually pres-

ent to the child. Hence, in the small *kvutzah*, the approach
to the child is easy and simple. But in the large settlements
there is a danger that the children will be as it were locked
up within the walls of their children's home. This is something which must not be permitted to happen if we want
the child to remain bound to the group, to the settlement
and its economy, to the work and to everything that we
hold dear. To achieve the desired aim, the commune must
be constantly aware of what is going on in the children's
home, and the life of the young ones must constitute a
matter of deep daily interest.

And now let us turn to the personnel occupying the key
posts in the process—those who are set over the child during this crucial formative period. We must face the truth
that this important function in the organism of the commune is entrusted too frequently to individuals with little
knowledge and experience. For the number of our children
keeps growing, and we have not concentrated on the problem of the children's home those energies and that devotion to which it is entitled.

The question of the right comrade in the children's home
is one of the most important in the settlement. She is responsible not only for the physical and mental condition of
the young, but also for the general atmosphere which dom-
inates the home and, in large measure, for the attitude of
the group toward the home. We have few working women
specialists in this line. In the course of time the woman in
charge learns much from the actual work, but there is,
meanwhile, a constant and heavy drain on her strength
and her nerves.

We shall establish our children's homes on true and
firm foundations only when we shall have prepared the
right number of skilled and devoted women comrades who
will know how to engage the interest of the entire settlement in their work. First we must make things lighter for
the woman in the children's home by improving her working conditions. The working hours must be shortened. (In

some of the *kvutzoth* the educator works ten and twelve hours a day.) The woman in charge of young ones must have a clear head, and must always be in the right mood. Further, the comrades must understand and appreciate the work of the educator; and the latter, after a time, must be given the opportunity to finish her training, either in Palestine or abroad.

A series of problems is raised by the kindergarten teacher. With children up to two years of age even the unskilled teacher may be used, for she hopes that her healthy, natural mother instinct will help her out, and that she will learn from the work itself. But it is otherwise with children between the ages of three and six, and none of our comrades would dare to accept the responsibility without the requisite training. And therefore the trained kindergarten teacher must be looked for outside of the commune, and this creates special difficulties.

In most cases the education of these girls is unsuited to our life and our form of community, and it is not easy to transplant them into the soil of a Palestinian communal group. The girl herself is assailed by a thousand doubts, and often the commune itself cannot help her; and it is the children who pay, in the end, for all these experiments. Often enough this situation simply has to be accepted. But the ultimate solution will be found when the settlements choose the right persons and then give them an opportunity to get the proper training.

And now something regarding the mother in her relation to our institutions—particularly the baby-home.

The woman who has lived for some years in the commune, and knows our institutions, certainly believes in this group upbringing as the best. And yet she suffers from a deep inner division. Nearly every woman wants to feed and tend her own little one. She wants to look at it every now and then, watch its daily development—particularly during that wonderful period of the first year. And if our mothers must surrender all this they suffer and long. Besides this, a mother trembles much more about the care of a new-born baby than about an older child, and with justice, because the first year of a child's life is the most important and the most dangerous. These denied emotions are responsible for the atmosphere of tension often to be found round our baby-homes. It is true that in most cases the mother has perfect confidence in the devotion of the women who work in the baby-home; and that confidence grows from year to year, it becomes mutual and is accompanied by understanding. And yet these difficult elements cannot be eliminated. They come most vividly to the fore when the child is sick. However strongly the mother controls herself, she still loses her peace of mind and her feeling of security. Her confidence in the comrade in charge weakens. She begins to make demands which, objectively seen, are inadmissible, and the two women cease to understand each other. At such moments we perceive the genuine difficulty of group unbringing for children, and we see ourselves lacking in self-training and self-control.

The struggle between intelligence and instinct emerges clearly in another case—when one mother comes to the help of another who can no longer give her baby milk. The possibility of this form of mutual aid is one of the strongest points in favor of our baby-homes. And the practice is a usual and accepted one. But sometimes it occurs that the child of the second mother needs more milk—and then it is very difficult for the first mother to ration her own child.

These are the details which make clear what goes on in the heart and mind of a mother who gives up her child to the group. It is unreasonable always to expect complete self-control; and we do wrong to accuse a mother of all sorts of weaknesses when this struggle is going on within her. This, indeed, is the moment for the most intimate kind of understanding.

The economic side of our children's homes has been the subject of much discussion, for this is the foundation of the whole system of group upbringing. Why is the cost so high for each child, and why do we need so many workers in the homes?

The majority of our group institutions are in the agricultural communes of the Valleys of Jezreel and the Jordan—and this is one of the reasons for the high cost of up-bringing.

Babies cannot be given cheap care in a climate which is hard even on grown-ups. The heat and the dryness are a strain on the children. In the summer months they lose their appetite, they vomit and run temperatures. Naturally not all of them suffer alike. Our climate bears hardest on babies which have just been weaned—that is, on babies between eight and eighteen months of age. The "older" ones, from two years on, gradually acclimatise themselves. When a child has been weakened by the great heat, it needs the special attention of a nurse if its later development is not to suffer.

There is another factor making for high costs. When a large number of children live in the same house the danger from infectious sicknesses increases. To combat this danger we have instituted a rigid system of hygiene, and this system, again, means money and personnel. And it is well to notice at this point that in times of epidemics in the country the children in our communes suffer less than all others. Official statistics also show that the infant mortality is lower in the group homes than among children brought up in individual families; they show further that our mortality rate compares well with that of the most developed countries in the world.

We are naturally doing what we can to reduce the costs; and in many of the *kvutzoth* they are considerably lower than they were a few years ago. But here again the possibility of advance depends in a large measure on the creation of a number of skilled and permanent child specialists. It is only through such workers that we shall improve our system; and it is up to all the comrades in the communes to help along. The collectivist workers' movement as a whole must create a common scientific institution for the solution of the problems of group upbringing for children.

Beth Alpha.   Nina Richter.

GROUP UPBRINGING AND THE CHILD

IT WAS before our marriages that we, the first women comrades in the communes, decided in advance that our children would be brought up in the group; not because we considered it a necessity of our life in the commune, but because we regarded it as a high ideal. Later, having become mothers, we still clung to this view.

We were proud and happy in the first trials of our strength and faith, in Deganiah, Kinereth and Tel Adas. Calmly, and in full consciousness of what we were doing, we chose the ablest of our women comrades for the task, and were prepared to entrust our children to her care while we went about our own work. Those first years exacted heavy sacrifices from us—of all the trials we underwent in the country and in the commune, this was the hardest and the most important. It will always remain so, for with every mother the old story begins anew.

Now, after these ten years of experience let us make an accounting and let us choose one standard of evaluation—the physical and mental development and well-being of the child.

It has become clear to us that for school children the richest and most harmonious form of upbringing is the children's home as it exists in our midst—not an isolated little world, but a children's community integrated with our own, growing with us, nourished with the spirit of our soil, lovingly cared for and watched over not only by the parents, but by the commune as a whole.

We have never thought of finding a substitute for parental love. We only wanted to add to it the love of the community, so that the child might never feel that when it steps out of its own home it is among strangers, needing protection. How much the first mothers in the communes suffered because of the false idea that parents must actually be alienated from their children! But, as the number of children and of parents grows among us, the old errors die out.

Even in the *kvutzah* the child without parents suffers, though it is known and felt in the children's home—from the comrade in charge down to the youngest one—that such a child must be treated with more tenderness than any other. Externally that child lacks nothing. But watch such an orphan closely! See him waiting eagerly for someone to come to *him* specially, and you will understand the pain which loneliness means even in the group form of upbringing.

For there are no bounds to the love which a child must have, so that its warmth may serve it through all the heavy after-life. And these children of ours, who will certainly inherit some of our burdens, do not look forward to an easy life.

Love and compassion alone can give us the strength needed to stand constant guard over the lives of our children, to listen with utmost patience to their needs and demands, to understand them without speech as long as they cannot speak for themselves.

And because among the comrades in charge, the nurses and educators, there are "many who are called, few who are chosen," difficulties must arise between them and the parents. We must bear in mind that the mother instinct of itself makes the mother a "chosen one" in respect to her child.

But this deep mother instinct no longer suffces to fill our lives, as it once sufficed for our mothers. I do not know whether it is good that this should be so, but so it is. The child does not, by itself, satisfy our life needs, does not answer all the demands which we make of ourselves.

And I also know that there is no road leading back to the one-time mother and one-time wife. Each of us women

must now tread her own path, and even the child cannot
hold us back. And if one of us should become weary, and
should want to turn back—she will find it impossible.
Those of us who still carry in their hearts the beautiful
idyll of the past, lose it when they have the chance to observe closely what has become of family life in the cities
today. . . .

And this consciousness that there is no road back, makes
the road before us all the harder.

And yet. . . .

    .   .   .

The hardest time in the life of the child, the period
which calls for the maximum care and worry in the mother,
is in the first three years. And when, a few days after the
birth, the mother must relinquish her child into other hands,
and cannot herself tend to all its needs, her sufferings begin.
For all these little cares and attentions are so important.
The new-born child changes from day to day—and the
progress is observed in all of these trifles, when the child
is being bathed, when it wakes from sleep, when it smiles
for the first time, and when the first glimmer of consciousness lightens in its eyes—in every movement, in every note
of its voice, it reveals itself anew.

And in the baby-home, even when it is developed to the
highest point, no one will wait for these little events with
the same eagerness and tenderness as a mother does.

But, on the other hand, it is impossible to estimate the
significance of the help which the baby-home gives the
mother when, ignorant, helpless and weak, she leaves the
hospital after her confinement. It is seldom that a young
mother in Palestine can fall back on a family with generations of tradition and experience to help her in her new
rôle. What substitute has this young mother? The book of
instructions? Not every woman has the time and the opportunity to read books; besides which, do we not know
how much help there is in a book when we have to face
realities—with a crying baby in our arms? Only those who

have seen for themselves what the lonely workingclass
mother must suffer, in the towns, or in the individualist
settlements, when her first child is born, can estimate the
worth of the baby-home for mother and child, can appreciate the value of its accumulated experience.

The baby home does not grope blindly through its problems, as even the educated and able mother often must.
Under the direction of the children-doctors and the devoted nurses they go forward with certain steps. But we
are worried constantly by one thought: how can we bring
into the life of the child which is being cared for in the
home, the bright glance and the loving smile of the mother
—for which even the tiniest creature instinctively longs?

It will be observed that when we compare the condition
of the children in the *kvutzah* with that of other workingclass children in Palestine and elsewhere, or even with the
condition of the children of other classes, we are perhaps demanding too much of the group method of upbringing. But we cannot forget what was in our minds
when we approached the whole problem at the beginning—
what ideals and wishes we had regarding life in Palestine
generally and our own lives in particular. For it is only as
part of a high cultural life that the group upbringing of
children has meaning, and only in the larger setting of a
general ideal will we find the strength to continue seeking,
through this form, a loftier and finer life for ourselves and
for our children.

Ain Charod.   EVA TABENKIN.

CHILDREN'S HOME AND PARENTS' ROOM

IF THERE were someone among us here, in the commune of Ain Charod, who could describe adequately what we have achieved in the way of group upbringing, it would afford much encouragement to those who are only just starting out on this road. Bit by bit our women workers in the children homes have ceased to be an isolated group working out its own salvation without the help of the other comrades. Today the entire commune follows with interest the progress of the children's homes. And bit by bit, too, we are establishing a harmony in the relations of our children to the group home and to the room of their parents.

The theory has been advanced that, in order to concentrate the impressions of the child, we must provide the children's home with so many comforts and attractions that the child will never feel the need of the room which is the home of its parents. But even if we had the means to carry out this theory to the limit, we should be doing wrong if we did not make possible *outside* contacts between children and their parents. Let our child get everything it needs from the specialists in the children's homes; let it spend the whole day there; but we *must* not put a check on the intimate meeting betwen child and parent. What these meetings mean in the life of the three—father, mother and child—must depend on their mutual relations. If we could turn our children's homes into palaces, I still would not relinquish that quiet, peaceful hour which I spend with my child in my own room, after the day's work, for the noisy public contact in the children's homes, in the presence of dozens of other fathers and mothers.

We have been convinced by observation that the more the child loves the room of its father and mother, the more it is satisfied by the life of the children's home. For after the exciting, strenuous day in the latter, the child finds by the side of its parents a deep tranquillity which is almost unknown to those children who grow up in private families.

But this restful evening visit raises another painful question. Is it right, after this hour of peace, to make the child return for the night to the children's home, to say goodnight to it and send it back to sleep among the fifteen or twenty others? This parting from the child before sleep is so unjust! In the morning that separation is natural. The sun shines, the child is bright and lively, it wants to run to its comrades, play with them, walk with them, work with them. As to the objection that it is bad for the child to sleep in the same room with its parents—can we not see to it that every family shall have two little rooms? Do we not, on the contrary, also know the dangers which beset children who sleep together in groups? A child sleeping at home is certainly sheltered from *these* dangers.

The women on the night watch in the children homes take turn and turn about. And when my turn comes to "go on guard" I feel my heart contract every time a child calls out in the night—sometimes out of its sleep, not knowing what it is calling—"Night-sister! Night-sister!" What is taking place in the soul of the child in that moment, between sleeping and waking? And who knows what is more important for the child, the conscious life of the day or the unconscious life of the night?

Ain Charod.   A. T.

MOTHERS' TALK

THIS is the day of judgment, when everyone is weighed in the balance—by "everyone," however, I mean only the children. The mothers stand in line outside the colony drug-store, waiting for their turn to use the scales. And waiting, they talk of all the homely details of their children's lives.

A mother comes out of the drug-store with shining face, her baby on her arms. Before she can say a word she is surrounded and overwhelmed with the question:

"How much?"

"Two hundred grams for the week!"

A few minutes later another comes out, her eyes darkened by sadness. Her four-month daughter is in her arms. We feel the pain at her heart, and we think it best to ask nothing. It is she who begins to speak.

"Three weeks my little girl hasn't gained a gram. And I'm to blame because I have to work in the garden and neglect the child. And I don't know—maybe I'm short of milk. I don't drink as much as I'm supposed to."

She goes on with her bitter self-criticism. The others comfort her. "You don't always have to blame yourself. You know that there are whole periods, in the summer, when the little ones just don't go forward. Even in the children's homes in the *kvutzoth* you have such cases. We're too impatient, and we get frightened too easily. . . ."

When the mother has gone, a hot debate sets in.

"Well, is it any better when the child goes to the kindergarten? We're not as scared about it—but we know it's already been spoiled at home. We always give way; we don't want the child to eat its heart out—and we haven't got the time to fight it out properly. And then we blame ourselves because we spoiled the child."

"And then the new worries, when the child begins to go to school. Will he grow up to follow in our footsteps? Will he have the courage and strength of will to continue our work. If at least he isn't any weaker than we are. . . ."

Other doubts crop up in the conversation. Ought we to give the child some work only when it asks for it, or ought we to demand its help, so that it may learn the duties of work early in life?

And another question: "Should we follow the old, traditional ways of our fathers and grandfathers and bring up our daughters differently from our sons? Or should we do the opposite? Perhaps it's all wrong to let the girl devote herself entirely to housework."

There is no clear answer to all these questions. We only know one thing. We, the older people, must observe scrupulously all the social rules and obligations which we have assumed in the settlement, so that the children may profit by example. However hard it is to leave the garden, the house and the little ones in order to live up to our standards of mutual help, it has to be done.

Things are hard today. Better times are coming, the children will be older, and beside the joy they bring us, they will also take a hand in the work.

K'far Ezekiel.   CHASIAH.

BORROWED MOTHERS

TAKEN as a whole, the inner struggles and the despairs of the mother who goes to work are without parallel in human experience. But within that whole there are many shades and variations. There are some mothers who work only when they are forced to; the husband is sick or unemployed, or else the family has in some other way gone off the track of a normal life. In such cases the mother feels her course of action justified by compulsion—her children would not be fed otherwise. But there are mothers who cannot remain at home for other reasons. In spite of the place which the children and the family as a whole take up in her life, her nature and being demand something more; she cannot divorce herself from the larger social life. She cannot let her children narrow down her horizon. And for such a woman there is no rest.

Theoretically it looks straightforward enough. The woman who replaces her with the children is devoted, loves the children, is reliable and suited to the work; the children are fully looked after. And there are even pedagogic theorists who say that it is actually better for the children not to have the mother constantly near them. As for the mother who is occupied outside the house—she of course has the great advantage of being able to develope. In any case, the ancient danger of retrogression is lessened; and therefore she can bring more to her children than if she were to remain at home. Everything looks all right. But one look of reproach from the little one when the mother goes away, and leaves it with the stranger, is enough to throw down the whole structure of vindication. That look, that plea to the mother to stay, can be withstood only by an almost superhuman effort of the will.

I am not speaking now of the constant worry that haunts the mother's mind that something may have happened. And I need not bring in the feelings of the mother when her child falls sick—the flood of self-reproach and self-accusation. At the best of times, in the best circumstances, there is the perpetual consciousness at the back of the mind that the child lacks the mother's tenderness, misses during the day the mother's kiss. We believe, above all, in education by example; and therefore we must ask ourselves: Whose is the example which is moulding the child of the working mother? A "borrowed" mother becomes the model. The clever things the child says reach the mother at second hand. Such a child does not know the magic healing power of a mother's kiss, which takes away the pain of a bruise. And there are times, after a wearying, care-filled day, when the mother looks at her child almost as if she did not recognise it; a feeling of alienation from her nearest and dearest steals into her heart.

And having admitted all this, we ask: Can the mother of today remain with her children? Can she compel herself to be other than she is because she has become a mother? That feeling of alienation between mother and child can occur, and does often occur in an even more serious form, when the mother always remains at home and cannot grow with her children. And the modern woman asks herself: Is there something wrong with me if my children don't fill up my life? Am I at fault if, after giving them, and the one more person nearest to me, a place in my heart, there is something left over which has to be filled by things outside the family and the home? Can we today measure devotion to husband and children by our indifference to everything else? Is it not often true that the woman who has given up all the external world for her husband and her children has done it not out of a sense of duty, out of devotion and love, but out of incapacity, because her soul is not able to take into itself the manysidedness of life, with its sufferings but also with its joys? And if a woman does remain with her children, and gives herself to nothing else, does that really prove that she is more devoted than the other kind of mother? And if a wife has no intimate friends, does that prove that she has a greater love for her husband?

But the mother also suffers in the very work she has taken up. Always she has the feeling that her work is not as productive as that of a man, or even of an unmarried woman. The children too, always demand her, in health and even more in sickness. And this eternal inner division, this double pull, this alternating feeling of unfulfilled duty —today toward her family, the next day toward her work —this is the burden of the working mother.

Tel Aviv.   **G. M.**

PART V
AMONG WRITERS

V

AMONG WRITERS

THE women of Palestine have their share in the literature of the country not less than their sisters of other countries. But in the case of the Jews the transition has been
more abrupt than elsewhere; until recently the mediæval
character of Jewish spiritual creation excluded the woman
almost completely.

The spiritual renaissance of the woman in Palestine is
part of the spring movement in the entire people; it has to
do with Zionism, with pioneering, with work on the earth,
with the rediscovery of the old-new land and the old-new
language, with socialist ideals. For this reason the majority
of our women who take a share in literary creation are intimately associated with those spiritual values which Palestine labor has inherited from the Jewish national and social movement, and which the woman has helped to
strengthen in thirty difficult years in the country.

The foremost characteristic of the work of these women
is its freshness. This springs in part from the newness of
the situation itself; we are not accustomed to hearing a
woman tell of herself in an art form; and we are affected,
too, by the newness of the woman's peculiar mastery of
the Hebrew language.

The jewish woman writer of Palestine devotes herself
chiefly to poetry and stories. The poetry volumes of the
last few years—by Rachel, Bath-Miriam, Esther Rab,
Elisheva, Anda Pinkerfeld—have made a place for the
Jewish woman in the Hebrew lyrical world. Among the
prose writers, Dvorah Baron is the only one who had established herself before she came to Palestine; but it is only

in Palestine that the following have come into their own—
Nechamah Puchatchevsky, Berachah Chabas, Shulamith
Kalugai, D. Abrahamith.

Not being able to reproduce here a complete anthology
of the literary product of Palestinian womanhood, we have
thought it proper, nevertheless, to reproduce in translation
at least some representative material from the lyrics of
Rachel Blowstein and the stories of Dvorah Baron.

Among the poets of Palestine none has achieved the tenderness and simplicity which characterise the two little
booklets *Saphiach* and *Mineged,* by Rachel. This work of
hers represents an extraordinary victory over the traditional burden of two thousand silent years, and a triumph
of the womanly spirit in Hebrew. She came to Palestine
knowing not a word of either Hebrew or Yiddish; and
perhaps this beauty was given to her because she sought
it in the Jewish village, in the commune, from mother earth
and from the Bible. But the lightness, naturalness and richness of her modest lines make one think rather of the great
Russian and European lyricists than of the typical Hebrew
poetry. It had to be a woman, and a "convert" who could
bring this new, refreshing spirit of nature into Hebrew
poetry. Still more strangely, the extraordinary gift of Rachel came to fruition only in the last part of her life, when
she lay sick of an incurable disease. Fastened almost constantly to her bed, she sent out her songs, which became
always deeper and more richly human as her body became
weaker and weaker. Her death took place in the spring of
1931.

Rachel came of a rich Jewish home which lived in the
heart of Russia, and was brought up in the Russian spirit in
a great city of the Ukraine. Dvorah Baron is the daughter
of a poor and distinguished father—a great Rabbi in a small
Lithuanian town—and she absorbed her Jewishness even
in the cradle. She has a profound Jewish knowledge, of the
type which few Jewish women were privileged to receive.
Rachel's poetry is all Palestinian; but in Dora's stories,

which appeared many years after she had settled in Palestine, there is not one which deals with the land itself. She was and remains one of the finest portrayers of the little Jewish town and its culture. Her best pieces measure up completely with the finest to be found in Peretz, Raisin and Ash. Her true, deep-rooted village-folk spirit comes to strongest expression in her hatred of the smug, contented life of the rich Jew and in her motherly compassion for whatever is abandoned, innocent and helpless. As artist she reaches her climax in the idealised pictures which she has drawn of her father and mother.

The symbolic picture of her father and of the Jewish mystery is contained in her story *The Genizah,* one of the deepest studies of man and of religion to be found in our new *belles lettres.*

The Palestinian woman of the new generation has her place in publicistic writing as well as in *belles lettres.* Almost everything that has appeared in the Hebrew press on the question of the woman, and her relationship to work, has been written by women. A *History of the Women Workers' Movement* has been written by Ada Fishman. From time to time women also write in the labor press and for the local, hectographed journals which appear locally. For the most part they are occupied with social and educational questions. We reproduce in this volume a woman's contribution to Palestinian publicist writing in the article *From Language to Language,* by Rachel Katzenelson which first appeared in the labor anthology *B'avodah,* in 1918.

R. K.

SONGS OF RACHEL

IDLE TALES

Red gleams the western sky as day begins to fail,
    And evening settles downward desolate and slow;
In such an hour the heart recalls an idle tale:
    "A little girl there was, long, long ago.

"A little girl there was, and young she was of will;
    Lightly she followed the plough from early until late;
And far across the fields she scattered grain until
    Her paths were closed by barricades of fate.

"The barrier stands forever about those joyous days,
    From earth's four corners now the ancient stormwind
        wails."
Oh evening! I am sated with your desolate ways.
    I will recall no more these idle tales.

PERHAPS

Perhaps these things have never been at all!
  Perhaps that life was not!
Perhaps I never answered morning's earliest call
  To sweat in labor on my garden plot!

Perhaps I never stood upon the loaded cart
  To gather up the hay,
Nor heard the wild songs bursting from my heart
  The livelong harvest day!

Perhaps I never made my body whole
  In the blue and quiet gleam
Of my Kinereth! Oh, Kinereth of my soul,
  Were you once true, or have I dreamed a dream?

IN THE GARDEN

Calm is the garden with blue and gray
   In the peace of dawn.
I will rise from the dust of yesterday
   To faith in the morn,
Accept with humble heart and free
The judgment that was given me.

A girl walks through the garden beds
   And scatters rain;
The withered leaves lift up their heads
   And live again.
The bitter things that God must do
I will forgive and start anew:

COMFORT ME

In both your dear hands, loving as a brother's,
  Take my own faltering hand.
You know and I know that the storm-tossed ship
  Will never make the land.

Comfort my tears with words, my only one;
  My heart is dark with pain.
You know and I know that the wandering son
  Will never see his mother's door again.

IN SICKNESS

To feel the darkness hammer on the eyeballs;
  To thrust blind fingers into empty space;
To start in terror when the bushes rustle;
  To pray for miracles and long for grace;

Seven times to hope what seven times was abandoned;
  From "Never, never," to "But a little wait";
To alternate 'twixt waking and oblivion;
  To curse my fate and to accept my fate;

To seek asylum in the lap of memory,
  To cling to her dear, loving folds in vain;
To shake with pain, or lie in drunken stupor
  Until the day breaks through the window-pane.

TO YOU

Morning and evening, toward you and you only,
  Toward you and you only my singing must strain;
Wounded or healed, rejoicing or weeping,
  In storm or in silence, in comfort or pain.

Instants may come when the magic seems broken,
  My vision is blinded, my compass untrue:
Sudden awakens my jubilant singing,
  Turns once again to its lode-star, to you.

To you and you only, of you and you only—
  My strings are a thousand, my song is but one:
In storm or in silence, in comfort or weeping,
  When sunlight is shining, when sunlight is gone.

BARREN

Oh, if I had a son, a little son,
With black, curled hair and clever eyes,
A little son to walk with in the garden
Under morning skies,
A son,
A little son!

I'd call him Uri, little, laughing Uri,
A tender name, as light, as full of joy
As sunlight on the dew, as tripping on the tongue
As the laughter of a boy—
"Uri!"
I'd call him.

And still I wait, as mother Rachel waited,
Or Hannah in Shiloh, she, the barren one,
Until the day comes when my lips will whisper,
"Uri, my son!"

MY MOTHERLAND

No deeds of high courage,
No poems of flame,
I bring you, my country,
To add to your fame;
By Jordan I planted
A tree in your soil,
And I wore out a path
In the field of my toil.

Well knows your daughter,
My own motherland,
How poor is her tribute,
How weak is her hand.
But my heart shouts with joy
When the sun shines upon you,
And in secret I weep
For the wrong that is done you.

THE GENIZAH

By Dvorah Baron

ON A sunny Sabbath afternoon of summer the Rav of
Zhuzhikovka stood on the pulpit before the sacred Ark,
and preached a sermon on the Weekly Portion from the
Book of Numbers, which had been read that morning at
prayers.

He told of Balak, son of Zippor, King of Moab, who had
been so terrified by the marvelous victories of the Children
of Israel over Sihon, King of the Amorites, and Og, King
of Bashan, that he did not go out to meet them in open war,
as befitted a King, but sent to Pithor for Balaam the Magi-
cian to curse them.

And before the listeners rose the strange picture of the
gentile prophet sitting on his ass in the narrow street with
a wall on either side—a narrow street not unlike the street
of the gentiles in Zhuzhikovka. And before the beast rose
suddenly the Angel of the Lord, so that in terror it pressed
close to the fence, almost crushing Balaam's leg.

Through the wide-open windows of the House of Prayer
on that hot summer afternoon, there came glimpses of the
neighboring meadow, which looked somehow greener and
younger than usual, because the hay had been mown just
a few days ago. And when the Rav told of the seven altars
which were raised in the field opposite the camp of Israel,
the eyes of his listeners turned quickly and involuntarily to
the huge stacks of hay which lifted up their rounded backs
to God's heaven.

But "no oppressor that riseth up against thee shall triumph," the Rav cried, in his leonine voice, and the folds of
his *talith* slipped downward from his shoulders, and flowed

proudly over the length of his silken mantle, right and left.

Then the Rav spoke with fierce power of the strength of the people Israel and its Torah, which is "a tree of life to those that take hold on it." And gradually he came nearer to the special content of the day's sermon, the two plans which he had for the Jews of Zhuzhikovka. The first was the ceremonious and reverential burial of torn books, fragments and defective Scrolls of the law, in a *Genizah*—after the ancient tradition of Israel which regards all printed and written paper on which the word of God has appeared, as eternally sacred, and entitled to decent interment when no longer in use; the second plan—more important—was the establishment of a little *Yeshivah* in the town of Zhuzhikovka.

But even before the Rav had reached the details of his plans, the faces of his listeners were illumined so brightly, that the two creases on his forehead—one for each plan—were at once smoothed out.

The Rav went on to mention "the days" which the poor students would have to eat in the houses of the various families of Zhuzhikovka, and then an excited murmuring and whispering came from the woman's section of the House of Prayer, and the rustling of old satin was heard for some minutes through the length and breadth of the House.

"What is there to think about? Are Mir and Volozhin, whose *Yeshivoth* are famous in all the corners of Israel, great cities? Are they not too, like Zhuzhikovka, little towns of hungry Lithuania?"

"Though thy beginnings be small, thy latter days shall be glorious!"—the words of the Rav flamed over his listeners, and he gathered together the corners of his *talith* in a last gesture of strength. Then he paused, being tired—for the sun had already sunk low and now stood over the river Zhuzhik—and passed on to the more beautiful part of his sermon, the parable; and the congregation, still trembling at the cry of his soul, breathed more easily.

With true affection the women looked at the young wife
of the Rav, where she stood in her dress of fine cotton with
its long waist, fitting close to her figure, when the Rav began to tell in glowing words of "that queen's daughter
whom everyone loved with a great love."

The golden wig on her head shone in the level rays of
the sun; and when, at the ending of the afternoon prayer,
she went down the steps from the women's gallery, and the
long train descended after her, step by step, raising a faint
cloud of dust, there was indeed a light as of royalty upon
her.

From the House of Prayer she turned down the narrow
street to the cool storage cellar, and drawing her dress together with a graceful gesture, she descended, like the other
women, to bring up the dairy dishes for the traditional
Sabbath evening meal. Meanwhile the Rav, his belt close
about him, stood near the well, talking with his intimates,
who had stopped there for a drink of water.

Now the last light of the sun died down and nothing was
left but a faint redness above the House of Prayer. The
meadow near by settled into a bluish darkness, and a faint
mist came up from the river Zhuzhik. The full-uddered
goats came back lazily from the pasture to drink their fill
in the lake.

They stopped awhile, like self-conscious beings, at the
end of the meadow, and then, without leader or guide, they
went down the narrow street in single file, and each goat
went straight up to its own house, and stood expectantly
before the big pail where—as it well knew—was prepared
its meal of rinds soaking in water, the peelings from the
threefold meal of the Sabbath Eve.

The summer was only at its beginning, and the vegetables had barely begun to ripen in that district, few being yet
obtainable in the market-place; nevertheless enough already
grew in the street of the gentiles to make up the modest
Sabbath evening meal of the Jews: little radishes, red or
white, when cut into pieces, soaked in sour cream and sprin-

kled with salt, make a dish not to be despised in lean Lithuania. One could also get, by this time, spring onions, to be eaten raw, whole or cut up, and dipped in vinegar, and perhaps a cucumber, chopped up and added more for taste than substance. There might also be red borscht, made from beet-roots, in which was dropped the yolk of an egg and the top of which was covered with a shimmer of cream. All in all, then, there was reason to thank God for the closing meal of the Sabbath in Zhuzhikovka.

And in fact, when the Rav's wife stood an hour later at the oven, preparing the "Farewell to the Queen"—that is to say, the Farewell to the Sabbath, the Royal Visitor— she was talking with her neighbor about these Lithuanian dishes. Her face lit up with its peculiar smile when she recalled how, when she first came into this district with her husband, she really could not look at these dishes, let alone eat them—and now she would not exchange them for the most elaborate dishes of Crown Poland.

She was still wearing the fine cotton dress with the long tight-fitting waist, but she had covered it with a house apron; in the neighbor's heart rose a motherly compassion, as she watched the little hands of the Rav's wife, shining white as they moved swiftly and lightly, peeling the big American potatoes.

When the coals in the three-legged stove began to glow, the young wife placed on them two Holland herrings, to roast. But she first set aside the roe to pour on the potatoes as appetiser—the year's store of pickled cucumber juice having already given out. Then she spread a week-day cloth on one half of the table and sat down to chat with her neighbor about the *Genizah*—the burial of the fragments of sacred books—which was soon to take place, right in the midst of the nine days of mourning between the first day of Ab and the Ninth, when the Temple was destroyed.

. . .

Early on Tuesday morning, when the Rav went down between the gardens to the old ritual bath-house, a heavy, dark mist still lay on the little street.

Dressed in his silk mantle, with the belt drawn tight, he passed, a tall, marvelous figure, through all the length of the big bath-house, between the two rows of up-ended benches and the faucets which dropped water on the idle willow-switches. He came to the little room which contained the tubs and the plunge.

Here he bent down to fix something in the stove, and lit himself a taper. Holding this in his hand he looked down doubtfully at the dark water in the plunge. Later, after he had dipped himself completely, he wrapped himself in a sheet by the light of the same taper and, though this was not the fitting place, he began to revolve in his mind the thoughts which he would weave into the sermon at the burial of the sacred fragments.

By now the windows of the bath-house, which had no shutters, were not as dark as before, and he could almost see the haystacks in the neighboring field.

On the narrow path, along which the goats went daily in single file, appeared suddenly the face of the bookbinder of Zhuzhikovka, who was carrying two bundles of newly plucked withes with which to adorn his street on the day of festivity. And all the sad verses which the Rav had thought of weaving into his burial sermon suddenly came to nothing.

The Rav dressed himself, and lit his pipe—it was the one which he usually smoked on Sabbath evenings—and went out through the street where stood the *hekdesh*, the shelter-house of Jewish wanderers. He came to the vestibule of the House of Prayer, and there the old sexton stood in the half-dark, surrounded by bundles and boxes of old fragments of books and parchments.

"Have they brought the clay pots?" the Rav asked, and drew at his pipe, so that his face glowed back with light; and he went closer to the boxes and bundles.

Here, among the bundles of torn parchment, there was a

package which he himself had brought last night from his old stores of books. He lit a candle and began to sort the torn leaves: fragments of the Kaballah in one heap, fragments of Religious Decisions in another; he even separated the fragments which came from the books of the Rambam, who is Maimonides, from fragments which came from the books of Rabad, who is Abraham ben David; for in their lives, many centuries ago, they had been opponents and had carried on a war of words, and they might not lie in peace together. But, doing this, the Rav thought it queer just the same.

This work done, the Rav clambered up into the attic, where lay hidden a Scroll of the Law which was defective by reason of an error, and several fragments of sacred parchment which had been defiled some time ago during the pogrom in the neighboring village of Semionovka. When the Rav came to the last step he paused, because the sexton who was lighting his way was weak, and the taper began to tremble in his hand; so waiting, the Rav extinguished his pipe and put it in the pocket under his mantle.

"Reb Motte," he asked the sexton, "has a burial of sacred fragments taken place in your days?" And he was astonished to see suddenly the golden sunlight poured out on the forest of birches beyond the town.

"Not in my days," the sexton answered with a sigh, as he felt with his foot for the last step. "But one took place in my grandfather's days." And he followed the Rav into the corner which was filled with the peculiar odor of dusty sanctities. He held up the candle, and they saw the old Ark with the wooden carvings, from the midst of which stared out—as if quite alive—the frightened face of the voiceless dove in the teeth of the lion: the parable of Israel among the peoples of the world.

"Wonderful, wonderful," the Rav whispered, straightening out his back, though he really did not know what was so wonderful; and yet the shudder which passed through all his body was more than he could bear. But the legend of the Talmud came to his mind: "As the dove stretches out its neck to the knife, and does not tremble, so Jews give up their lives for their sanctities." And as the words went through his mind, confused and dark, he opened the drawer above the Ark, where lay the fragments of parchment saved from the pogrom of Semionovka.

But suddenly the sexton sprang back in terror and cried out:

"Rabbi! Rabbi! She is naked!"

"Who?" the Rabbi asked, startled, and did not recognise his own voice, which sounded so dead and brought back no echo from the walls.

"The Glory herself!" The sexton lowered the taper and they saw the little Scroll of the Law, naked indeed, without velvet mantle and without cover. The Rav slowly lifted the scrolls by the handles which are called trees of life, and placed the Torah tenderly under his cloak, like a father taking his child to his breast. He went downstairs perturbed, feeling with his feet for the steps. At the foot of the stairs already waited the first prayermen.

.   .   .

Minah—the old childless widow Minah—who came from the family of priests, the Sons of Aaron, had risen specially early on this day, so as to lead her goat to pasture before the first quorum of praying men was through.

But it fell out otherwise, and by the time she had come back from the shed, had passed the milk through the sieve and had boiled it, the rays of the sun were already on the copper tray which stood on the shelf of her room. Nevertheless she put on her dress of stiff satin, which rustled with a sound of proud generations long dead, put her wimple on her head, drawing out both points (she had to do this without a mirror, being without one) and took out from under the rafter—God help her, she was only a woman!—a bundle of leaves belonging to an ancient Bible Reader printed, alas, in plain Yiddish! An inheritance it was, the remnants of the book from which her grandmothers and great-grandmothers had read, being unable to read Hebrew like the menfolk. And this was Minah the widow's contribution to the collection of sacred leaves which the village was to bury in pomp. Quickly she took up the bundle, went out of the house, and locked the door behind her.

She perceived at once that she could not have chosen a more unfortunate moment. For just then there came, out of the house opposite, the President of the Synagogue. He wore a coat of wool, drawn close about him; behind him came his two sons, and each one carried a bundle of genuine fragments, remnants of illustrious and scholarly books, and no pitiful make-believe stuff like her own.

Her heart sank within her. But she went on. In one hand she held the rope which was tied to the horns of the goat which followed her along the narrow street, and in the other she carried the bundle of dubious documents. She came at last to the well, tied the goat to the post, and, bent deeper than before, turned toward the women's entrance of the House of Prayer.

A crowd of young rascals blocked her path, and threatened to untie the goat and ride it through the town.

"Look! look!" they yelled in chorus, "Minah's got a book; look, look, Minah's got a book!"

In the House of Prayer the second group had ended its devotions, and the worshippers were out on the street. In her extremity Minah the widow fled into the vestibule, and there she perceived the Rav, who was standing by the boxes of manuscript, splendid in his mantle. And it seemed to her that she had escaped out of a flaming desert into the shadow of a cool grove.

"Make way for Minah, of the family of the priests!" the Rav cried, stretching out a hand to take the bundle of fragments from her.

Before his eyes there had appeared, as if revealed by a lightning flash, the image of the widow who, many, many

centuries ago, had brought a handful of meal to lay upon
the altar, and he heard the voice which declared to the
priest: "Despise not her offering, for it is as if she had
brought her soul to lay upon the altar." And the eyebrows
of the Rav trembled, and he looked down into the box of
fragments.

         .   .   .

In an hour's time the work had so far progressed that
they could send the draymen for the horses which were
out to pasture.

When the thirty clay pots had been filled with fragments,
covered, and set out in a row, the old sexton laid on them
an old altar curtain. Suddenly Baruch Brenn—the oldest
and most respected householder in the town, and the second scholar to the Rav himself—remembered that in his
house, behind the big cupboard, there was a bundle of sacred "Questions and Answers" which his grandfather—
his soul rest in peace!—had put there years ago. And eager
to do the good deed himself, and bring these fragments, too,
to decent burial, he set out at a run for his home, his coat
tails lifted behind him, flying so fast that even his grandsons could not keep pace with him.

Now the musicians were instructed to range themselves
in two rows, and the draymen—a father and his son—
mounted on the box of the cart. They had neither whip
nor switch in their hands, and they turned their horses
down the alley which lies between the House of Prayer and
the market-place.

A shy smile hovered on the face of the Rav's wife when
she came into the yard of the House of Prayer, dressed in
a woolen dress, and with a light, transparent shawl on her
shoulders. Most of the women, true housewives of the
town, wore the accepted holiday uniform of Zhuzhikóvka,
a stiff satin dress covered by a pleated apron and a smooth
black wimple with two points which stuck out and trembled as they walked.

But when the assembly reached the market-place, and

the musicians began to play on their instruments—two drums, a trumpet and a violin which pierced to your insides—no one had a mind any more for the dresses and wimples of the women.

Earnestly and solemnly, as conscious of their own importance as were the young oxen of Samuel the Prophet which brought the Holy Ark from the field of the Philistines to Beth-Shemesh, the horses strode across the marketplace between rows of closed shutters through the clouds of dust and the excited crowd. Great was the astonishment of the Russian postmaster and the clerks of the town hall, who followed the procession with uncovered heads and staring faces as far as the cemetery itself; and there the voice of the Rav—and the voice was enough!—changed the look of amazement on their faces to one of indefinable terror.

But the voice of the Rav was enough to make anyone tremble. There he stood wrapped in his prayer-shawl. A faint green lustre was on his face. He spoke of the marvelous and eternal union of souls between Israel and the Torah. He also spoke of the time of the redemption, when all the dead would rise to life; at that time, he recalled, the sacred fragments which they were burying now would also rise.

"And I will open your graves and I will lift you up and I will bring you unto the Land of Israel,"—and the Rav stretched out his hand now over the graves and the monuments of the fathers, and now over the stones and wooden headpieces of the children; and it seemed that a sigh came from the trees which shook themselves and bowed their heads.

Oh, this was no longer the village of Zhuzhikovka, which the young people had been abandoning during the last few decades, in favor of the great world outside. No! Here stood a congregation of Israel, four hundred years old, headed by a long line of fifteen illustrious Rabbis, adorned with families of the Priests, descendants of Aaron, and sanctified by the presence of martyrs who had died for the Name of the God of Israel; and in this transformation a cry of mourning, altogether unlike the mourning of bereaved ones, rose over the holy field and lingered above the heads of the assembled.

Baruch Brenn, the greatest scholar among the householders of the town, had laid his barred kerchief across the gravestone of his father, and pressed against it his face which was distorted with sobbing; and Minah, of the family of the Priests, had pushed her way through to her "portion," the four ells of earth which she had bought herself next to the grave of her husband, and there she threw herself on the grave of her husband and clung convulsively to the grass, just as if she did not have a little house of her own, with a little barn to the side, in the middle of the town and a milch goat on the pasture behind the House of Prayer.

But just at this point the Rav ended his sermon with the dry, closing formula *Uvo l'Zion Goel, Amen,* and, stepping forward, was the first to throw a spadeful of earth on the manuscripts in their grave.

In groups the congregation drifted down behind the musicians toward the ferry, and there, on the edge of the river, while the trumpet was pealing and the fiddle was singing, they saw the Rav step up to the old drayman and, giving him his hand, exclaim heartily, "Happy journey!"

"He's going to Tuchanovka, to bring the first Talmud students!" This was clear to everyone who beheld how the face of the Rav lit up, while the wind lifted playfully the points of his mantle. And they stood, petrified and silent, watching the drayman erect on his cart disappearing slowly among the fields of wheat which lay on his right and left.

FROM LANGUAGE TO LANGUAGE

By Rachel Katznelson*

I

It was in Kinereth, during one of our comradely conferences, that I first clarified in my own mind the two concepts: revolutionary movement and revolutionary literature.
It was then too that I became conscious of the revolutionary character of Hebrew literature and began to understand why we had passed from Yiddish to Hebrew and
wherein, for us, lay the difference between these languages.

Fifteen years ago we began, of our own free will, to
speak Yiddish just as later, of our own free will, we began
to speak Hebrew. I believe that we have not as yet evalu-
ated the significance of this period in our lives. We were
then just a handful of people (in Palestine too we learned
not to become enthusiastic about numbers) who felt that
we *had* to begin speaking Yiddish. The language was
like a homeland in exile. Every word we uttered in Yiddish seemed to be a reminder of a home—a street, a labor
group. This mystery of being Jewish lived for us only in
the poverty-stricken hovels; somehow it seemed contrary
to sense to believe that in the houses of the rich there were
Jews too. The secret and the beauty of the race lay for us
in the little children's faces on the streets of the poor. On
summer evenings we walked in those streets to listen to
the murmur of the thousands of voices of the workers,
just as we might have walked in the forest to hear *its*
thousand voices. We felt that here was life. The first
time we listened to a reading in Yiddish the whole of this
world was unveiled to us. Then we found the writers
of this world, too, Morris Rosenfeld, Peretz and the

*Rachel Katznelson Shazar

younger ones of our own generation; the simplicity of
Abraham Raisin appealed to us only later, and last of all
we unlocked the door that opened on the riddle of Sholom
Aleichem.

Every Yiddish word, spoken or written, that was
touched with emotion, youth or art, we received in us as
if it were a separate greeting from home. The language
was new to us, and therefore poor in vocabulary, and
yet we never felt "a lack of words." This was perhaps
the one short period in our lives when our speech was dominated by truth. The language was indeed poor, and each
one of us knew two or three richer languages, but all our
inmost life found, without seeking, its full expression in
Yiddish. For the first and perhaps only time we felt the
pride of language and of its music, knew that this tongue
was an intimate secret between ourselves and our people,
knew that for every experience of the soul an expression
had been prepared, and that this expression lay stored up
somewhere, ready to be called into instant use. And how
we used to suffer when someone spoke a false, artificial
Yiddish! We simply could not understand how anyone
could be unaware of the un-authenticity of that speech—
with all those good teachers around him.

Many of us, particularly among the young, knew Hebrew, too. Interest in Hebrew awakened almost simultaneously with interest in Yiddish. But for most of us
the knowledge of Hebrew was a dead or paralysed thing.
Even those who did not know Hebrew felt that in this
language too there lay a great national treasure, and they
wanted to learn about it. This was the time when Bialik's
poetry was shaking the Hebrew world. His "City of
Slaughter," the song of pain and rage awakened in him
by the massacre of Kishineff, and his "Pool" had recently
appeared. To the ears of those who could not read Hebrew
came nevertheless the news of the existence of such poets
and writers as Chernichovsky, Feierberg and Shofman.
They were translated and read. But it occurred to none

of us to want to speak Hebrew; Yiddish seemed to us our natural medium of speech. And how could we turn from a natural to an artificial medium?

Yet it was this deep and natural bond which we severed on coming to Palestine. None of us here feels any longer that he is a child of Yiddish! And when we speak Yiddish sometimes, or hear it spoken, and listen with joy to the sure, unfaltering words, it gives us such pleasure as one may feel in hearing someone speak a language well, having all its secrets at his command—yet not a language to which we are intimately bound! The passionate attachment to Yiddish no longer exists for us. We master the language, but it does not master us.

For this betrayal we paid dearly, as one pays for every betrayal. And yet we had to make the betrayal and pay the price. And we feel the need to explain and make clear to ourselves why this had to happen.

The fact that Hebrew was the old national language could not influence us; such theoretical considerations have never prompted people to leave a living tongue. Nor could we be influenced by the fact that there are Jews in the world who do not understand Yiddish and that Yiddish is declining. After all, there are many Jews who do not know Hebrew either. And if there are some who are forgetting their Yiddish, there are others who are just beginning to love it. Moreover, are we not the children of our generation, and is not our principal concern the consciousness of being true to ourselves and achieving inner peace? Certainly the fact that we were few in number (we were fewer when we turned to Yiddish than when we turned to Hebrew) meant nothing to us. We had seen with our own eyes how minorities grow to majorities. Nor could we be bribed by the richness of Hebrew. For, in the first place, what had become of that richness? It was not apparent in the Hebrew we spoke. Was it not a dead language, without a soul, filled with strange expressions and a strange spirit? And was not every beautiful Hebrew expression a sort of miracle to us? And in the second place, "poverty is no shame," and the poor man loves even his bit of poverty—his true possession.

How was it, then, that we so swiftly threw overboard that which had been the very content of our lives?

II

When we consider the hopes which our generation reposed in the Yiddish language, and the respect which we felt for Hebrew, it seems that the division of the writers between Hebrew and Yiddish should have been other than it actually was. J. Ch. Brenner should have written his stories of Yiddish town life in Yiddish, while Ash should have written his idyll of the Jewish village in classical Hebrew. What happened was the opposite. And it was characteristic of the young generation of writers, Yiddish and Hebrew, who were brought up on the same street, often as boyhood friends, and knew both Yiddish and Hebrew, that they should part company in this fashion. Brenner, Shofman and Gnesin wrote only in Hebrew; Raisin, Einhorn and Nistor only in Yiddish. The difference between these groups began only when it came to the choice of language, and this was dictated by an organic, inner impulse. We must bear this in mind when we examine the question as a whole.

A language has its own atmosphere. It is impossible to learn a language thoroughly without being influenced by its spirit. For the language is the storehouse of a people's energy. The history of the people—not the written history alone, but the history which has been lived and felt, the totality of its aspirations and experiences— is enclosed forever in its language. He who knows the people, its history and its language, knows at once what words have their peculiar sound and sense, such as cannot be found in another language. And this peculiarity of sound or timbre is related to a specific characteristic of the people, or to a specific incident in its history, or to a specific association born of its utterance by a national hero in a moment of crisis. The memory of the people is loaded with these expressions of exceptional circumstances, some national catastrophe, a moment of national religious ecstasy, of national danger, of national creativity. And even though only a handful were present when the expression was coined or the word uttered, the sound of it is carried like seed across the length and breadth of the people.

But it is not only the unusual that leaves its mark on the language; the usual, the ordinary also wear their grooves, and therefore a language continues to grow as long as people speak it and think it. And the richer our inner life is, the richer is the heritage we bequeath to the language, the richer the atmosphere in which we move, and in which those coming after us will move. The words which we have used to convey deep thought and feeling will have had their effect on someone; he will never be able to use those words again without remembering what we have put into them. And the converse is also true; every flabby or stereotyped thought impoverishes the spirit and lowers the level of the people.

Every language has its magic circle, within which the listener—once he has entered the circle—becomes sensitive to the echoes of all words. Anyone who has mastered several languages thoroughly knows how one changes with each new language. For a language is not merely a collection of words and expressions; it is the whole of the past in living form.

"In times of doubt, in days of dark thoughts for the fate of my fatherland, you, my language, are my only support. Only you, our vast, powerful, true, free Russian speech! For it is imposible that so mighty a language should have been given to any but a mighty people." (Turgeniev, *The Russian Language.*)

Every language has its own boundaries and limitations, according to the intellectual and emotional stores it contains. And these limitations determine the heights which the language can attain. Beyond this height the artist himself cannot reach. And the converse is again true: no expression can sink lower than a given limit for a given language.

The heavier the heritage is, the more difficult the life. The children of a people with a great past do not fit easily into the ways of life; because a language exacts as well as endows. But Jews have never declined this difficulty; they have continued to increase their heritage.

The national energy which is deposited in the Hebrew language has not ceased to live through the thousands of years in which Jews have not spoken the language. Religion was its guardian. It is perhaps because of this religion that, after two thousand years, Chernichovsky should have been able to write in Hebrew. The religious life filled and refilled the heart of the Jewish people with perpetually renewed confidence, flooding every corner of it with spirit; it was this religious life which returned to the Hebrew language that intimacy of which it had been deprived by the other language—the language of the home and street. And *per contra*, the religious idea (either in the form of philosophy, or of science, or of poetry—everything was then religion) was strengthened from the inexhaustible sources of the Hebrew language. In this beneficent interaction the life of the people, touched always with new concepts, new intentions and new secrets, was carried from generation to generation.

And here our people has been speaking Yiddish for several hundred years, and in this language too we have accumulated great stores of national energy. We are fed, from these stores in their various forms—the mother, childhood, our history in exile, things that are true and dear and belong to us. And these are the two worlds which lie before the young generation of Jewish writers.

In the time through which we are living our national possessions have become dearer than ever to us; and our pride will not permit us to treat with contempt one of our high possessions simply because it is not perfect and harmonious. And only in a time of such jealous love could the war of languages have broken out in our midst in the manner which it actually assumed. But we should know that if a writer has made his definite choice of one of the languages and not of the other, it was not through accident; he has merely obeyed an inner command, itself the inevitable result of his relationship to the tradition which the language contained. Each one of us carries on the tradition of the language in which he lives, not knowing it and sometimes even not willing it.

III

When we tried to characterise the original Yiddish literature we used to say: "The Yiddish literature is more national than the Hebrew." What we wanted to say was that the warmth which we felt in the Yiddish literature was absent from the Hebrew. It was in Yiddish that we were loved as we were, in the Jewish street and the Jewish village. And this was one of the main virtues of Yiddish.

A Yiddish writer on a Warsaw newspaper once made the round of the Jewish villages within the Pale, and found in each setttlement treasuries of poetry—in the life of the places, in their inhabitants, in their past. This would have been impossible in the Hebrew literature; even Levinsky would have been unable to find it.

The impression produced on us by Peretz's Yiddish *Folk Tales* was in its way not less profound than that produced by Bialik's Hebrew *City of Slaughter*. In our hearts we gave all these stories one name: "Devotion unto Death," for this was the poetry of our martyrdom, and our faithfulness in exile.

The relationship of Yiddish literature toward us was like that of a mother who, out of deep love for her child, is unable to understand its inner struggles, its faults and complexities, simply because it is her child and she is only the mother.

And in those years, soon after the first Russian Revolution, when everything within us was so tense, we felt in Yiddish literature something too soothing, something that holds down the wings, something that prevents one from drawing deep, free breath.

There was a time when the Jewish village was to us what it was for Sholom Ash: a world in itself, locked in, sustaining itself in its own beauty. But this was not what we now needed. If it had been possible for us to see Jewish life only as it was mirrored in the Yiddish literature, we could not have considered ourselves a great people.

There is a touch of bitterness in what I want to say about Yiddish—the bitterness of a dillusioned first love, which leaves behind it, together with its pain, the clear realisation that the early freshness of relationship which is found but once in life is gone forever. And even the knowledge that Yiddish bound us to the life of the people and helped us to remain true to it can no longer console us.

Great and honest talents belonged to Yiddish. But why was it that only the Hebrew literature could restore to us the feeling of self-respect? Why was Yiddish utterly devoid of that hypnotic power which characterised a Bialik, a Feierberg, a Gnesin? It is not a question of talent, but of personality. The magic of Hebrew was in the freshness of its people; and it was for living persons that we longed. For us Bialik's song, *The Branch Sank Down*, Chernichovsky's introduction to the translation of *Hiawatha*, the problems in Feierberg, and women and nature as they appeared in Gnesin—were *human*, personal utterances. And where there are persons, there the folk is. But the Yiddish literature was touched throughout with modesty, softness, and the fine eroticism and love which had flooded the Yiddish writing in Poland. This love, which is to be found in the Yiddish stories of Chassidism, and in Ash's *The Village*, and which accounts perhaps for the magic of Peretz's *Folk Tales*—this love may possess the power to uncover the secrets of life and to create a complete life philosophy. But there are times in the life of a people, and in the life of a man, when nothing is more dangerous than the idyllic and the intellectually narrow. Such a time had come for us, in fact, when each of us had to find his own answer to the question of a language.

A wide gulf lay between the actual difficulty which faced the individual Jew and the manner in which this difficulty was treated in the Yiddish literature and press of the time. (By "the Yiddish literature and press of the time" I mean the main current of Yiddish writing, and not that small part of it which was a reflex of the Hebrew literature and press.) On the one hand the reforms which certain Yiddishist writers (protagonists of Yiddish) wanted to introduce into our life wounded us by their tactlessness and lack of comprehension—like the interference of a stranger in one's most intimate affairs. Who of us has forgotten, for instance, the solemn debates on the subject of substituting Latin for Hebrew letters, or of dropping Hebrew from the curriculum of the Jewish schools? And on the other hand there was a kind of terror when we spoke of national affairs in Yiddish, a fear of taking a free step lest the old dress we wore would rip apart. Yiddish was conservative, and could only see the things of the immediate hour.

Only in Hebrew literature and in the best Hebrew literature, did we feel ourselves freed from the yoke of the national censorship which crushed Yiddish literature everywhere. Here people could speak freely about themselves, about Jews, about the world at large—and it was thus that Achad Ha-Am, Berditchevski and Bialik spoke.

Our nationalism interfered with our life. Thought and emotion were pointed only to one end, and we lacked the freedom of other human efforts. Every enthusiasm for general, not specifically Jewish matters, pulled us or tried to pull us closer to the alien world. It was impossible to be a socialist, a Tolstoyan, an artist, a politician or a scien-

tist without the fear of falling a victim to assimilation. If
you took one step toward human freedom, you felt yourself alienated from your people; one step toward social
interests—alienation again. And that was why, in the fierce
impulse toward Palestine, we also felt the fierce impulse
to get rid of the *idée fixe* of nationalism. For in Palestine
we would be Jews *anyhow*—and that was what we
wanted. It was this assurance that we found in the Hebrew language. In this language the writer feels himself
more a citizen of the world than he does in Yiddish. His
national certainty is stronger in it, his consciousness of his
own peculiar character deeper-rooted; and therefore he
feels a wider freedom in it, too. In this language he feels
that, whatever he does, whatever interests he has, whatever activities he pursues, he still spins in a mysterious way,
tacitly, and without attention, the eternal thread of his
people.

IV

The revolutionary character of the Hebrew literature is
revealed both in its affirmations and in its negations.

Two years after the appearance of the *Folk Tales*,
appeared Brenner's *Mikaan U-mikaan*. I wonder if Brenner
ever suspected that his book would be a deeper and richer
well of hope and security than the *Folk Tales*. In any
case, we felt one thing: if a man could write about us—as
Brenner did—without the slightest touch of pity, it was a
sign that we still lived. And the hope with which he pre-
sented us in *Mikaan U-mikaan* is our only one—but our
true one. It was just at this moment, too, that the Yiddish,
the Russian-Jewish, and even a part of the Hebrew press
were dominated by such a spirit of caution, of timidity and
of apology that they seemed to be concerned not with a
living people, concerning which one may speak freely, but
a dead people, concerning which one may say only the
kindliest, most meaningless things.

But the power of Hebrew lay in something more than
its negations. There are great negators whose lives have

been one great affirmation. And there are some men who
are so secure in themselves that they do not need the tonic
of negation. Such a one was A. D. Gordon, who issued
his challenge to Brenner's savage analysis of Jewish reality.

Another great affirmer of life was Feierberg, who was
something more than a mere guide. Most of us have not
yet learned to evaluate him properly. And it is indeed difficult to grasp him. If Bialik, for instance, had written only
for three years, would we have known anything about him?
But even in the stammering of the young Feierberg—for
all his speech, concentrated flame and passion though it is,
is only a stammering in comparison with what he had to
tell us—there is hidden something that has no parallel in
Hebrew literature. His stories have a natural power of attraction because there was, between him and Jewish history, a type of relationship which no one else had. If he
had lived long enough to write the life of the Baal Shem
Tov, as he intended to, he would have given us a new vision
of Chassidic and Jewish history, and not the cleverly
thought out, artificial stories of Chassidism which (in
comparison to Feierberg's relationship to Jewishness) are
Peretz's.

And thus the spirits came to the parting of the ways.
Had Brenner at least written in Yiddish, the picture would
have been different; not simply because another great
talent would have been added to Yiddish literature, but
because the incident itself would have been symptomatic.
But the division of talents took place so clearly and un-
mistakably, all our dissatisfaction with our life of today,
all our demand for a complete change swung over not to
the "living" language, but to the "dead" one!

Yiddish was the language of the folk, of democracy; but
in Yiddish literature there reigned narrowness, inertia and
—as seen by our generation—the spirit of reaction. The
stream of thought which meant revolution for us found
its expression in Hebrew literature. And every person
of living thought—and this is truest for the children of

our generation, cur people and our situation—feels himself drawn toward the sources of revolution.

Jerusalem, 1918

ILLUSTRATIONS

Deganiah at its birth in 1910

K'far Gileadi (1930)

A corner of Deganiah (1932)

In the Girls' Training Farm at Nachlath Jehudah (1930)

Children of Ain Charod on an outing (1930)

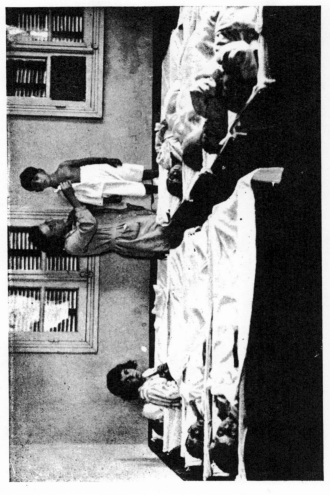

Children's Home of the Council of Women Workers in Chederah, founded 1930

Rachel Blowstein

EPILOGUE

By Beba Idelson

Those interested in knowing what became of the *haverot* (comrades) who contributed their stories to the original edition of *The Plough Woman* can find some of them spending their old age in kibbutzim, moshavim and cities; a few are now residents at homes for the aged; many are no longer among the living. But in this book, which is a personal and intimate account, they not only left us memories of their personal aims and struggles and a collective image of women rich in spirit and ready to make any sacrifice for their ideals, but they also succeeded in expressing the spirit of an entire era.

The period they describe, starting with the Second Aliyah which began during the first decade of our century, witnessed a one-time miracle: the renascence of young Jews returning to their ancient land to create a new society.

Nearly half a century has passed since *The Plough Woman* was first published. Since then, endless changes have taken place in the world, in Israel and in the Working Women's Movement, but that unique period left an indelible mark, and it still forms the foundation on which our movement built and has continued to shape its activities to this day. The same spirit of endeavor and dedication still marks every phase of our work today.

During these past decades, our movement has absorbed hundreds of thousands of *haverot*. Some came to Israel as *halutzot*—pioneers—after *hachsharah* on training farms in the diaspora; others prepared for their new life at *mishke poalot*—women workers' farms—which we set up for them in Israel. Others, later on, came as survivors of the Holocaust, bringing with them the

BEBA IDELSON served as general secretary of the *Moetzet Hapoalot* (Working Women's Council) for over four decades until her retirement in 1975. She was elected to Israel's Parliament in 1949, serving as Deputy Speaker from 1955 to 1961. She is the author of numerous articles on the problems of working women.

agony of the death camps, or the heroism of participation in partisan and resistance groups. To all these, the Working Women's Movement gave guidance and assistance in their various paths towards absorption in the Homeland.

As time went by, the Working Women's Movement established a remarkable network of branches and institutions, covering the entire land of Israel—in cities, villages, kibbutzim, moshavim, development towns and workers' settlements. We now have more than 600,000 members and maintain over 1,000 institutions and have thus become an important factor in the life of the country. In our institutions and kibbutzim we have helped absorb boys and girls who were torn from the arms of their parents and who finally found a warm and loving home with us in Israel. We have also raised and educated children from underprivileged homes in Israel, helping them to find their way to a wholesome life, thus narrowing the social gap in the country.

Our movement has also done its share in the defense of the Homeland. We stood up to Arab riots which afflicted us at various periods and endured four wars of survival. Our *haverot* took an active role in *Hashomer,* the group which guarded the early settlements, *Haganah,* the defense force of Palestine Jewry, and the *Palmach* commando units. During World War II, some of our members joined the British Auxiliary Territorial Service (A.T.S.) to help in the Allied war effort. Since the establishment of the State, our *haverot* have served in *Chen,* Israel's Women's Army Corps, *Nahal,* which helps till the soil and defend the land, and the civil defense corps, which guards and defends life and property in our towns and cities.

During this entire period we continued to educate women toward equality and independence, toward acquiring a profession and becoming active in public life, and toward the role of equal partners in the structure of the country in general and the labor movement in particular. We have also aided Arab women in Israel in achieving personal and social progress; some of them have, in fact, become active in our movement.

We have been concerned also with the civic and political position of women. Since the establishment of the State of Israel, our *haverot* in the Knesset, Israel's Parliament, have been instrumental in the enactment of many laws to advance the status of women in society, at work and in the family. Our legislative achievements have placed Israel in the front ranks of the enlightened nations of the world and have strengthened our appearances on the international scene.

Ours is the only women workers' movement in the world that numbers among its members not only women who are working outside the home for pay but also housewives who are not part of the labor force. The latter have become an important factor in our movement through their own group, *Irgun Imahot 'Ovdot* (Working Mothers' Organization), making their distinct contribution in culture, education and social service as volunteers.

From its dynamic beginnings, Pioneer Women in the United States and Canada, our sister organization in the Diaspora, has grown into a strong movement with branches in twelve countries. Together with the Working Women's Movement in Israel, it is the largest women's organization within the Zionist movement. It supports us in our immense task of creating a better society from the melting pot of immigrants ingathered in the Jewish Homeland. The educational and cultural activities of Pioneer Women in the Diaspora communities have been an important factor in Jewish life outside Israel.

All these and other achievements make up a glowing canvas which justified our celebrating, with satisfaction and pride, the fiftieth anniversary of the *Moetzet Hapoalot* (Working Women's Council) two years ago, and now, in 1975, the jubilee of the Pioneer Women's movement in the Diaspora.

The English title of this book, *The Plough Woman*, conveys a two-fold meaning: literally, the desire of the early *halutzot* to become tillers of the soil as a primary basis for the healthy existence of a nation, and symbolically, the cultivation of a new society in a rebuilt Homeland.

Both these meanings are still valid today. Even though agriculture plays a relatively small role in the modern economy, the agricultural settlements continue to be an influential and inspiring element in Israel, and our movement has continued its work of "ploughing" in the sense of education and guidance with the same fervor as in the early days.

268

The early pioneering days are long past, but they are still fresh in the memory of our movement, and they continue to inspire its activities. They will continue to serve as guidelines to us and to future generations, as women and as members of the Israeli and worldwide Labor Zionist movement, striving for the rebirth of our own nation and a creative life in a peaceful world. Therein lies the value of *The Plough Woman*.

Last, but not least, we wish to express our tribute of admiration to our *havera* Rachel Katznelson Shazar, who edited this book and who served as an inspiration to the women whose names appear as contributing authors in *The Plough Woman*.

1975

APPENDIX

THE EDITOR

THE CONTRIBUTORS

PERSONALITIES

PLACES AND TERMS

THE EDITOR

Rachel Katznelson Shazar

The life of Rachel Katznelson Shazar—pioneer, teacher, editor, literary critic, labor leader and President's wife—has spanned almost nine decades. Born in 1888 in Bobruisk, Russia, she was raised in a well-to-do, highly intellectual family. After completing high school, she began to study Hebrew and soon joined the Labor Zionist movement.

In 1912 she settled in Palestine, and taught evening courses at the girls' agricultural training farm which had been founded at Kibbutz Kinneret by Hanna Meisel-Shochat.

At Kinneret, she first became active in organized efforts to further the welfare of the young working women who had come to Palestine to rebuild the Jewish Homeland. She became a leading figure in the struggle of Jewish working women for equal rights with men and in the search for adequate ways to care for the children of the settlements while their mothers worked in the fields.

Before long, however, Rachel Katznelson felt the need to participate personally in the actual work of pioneering. She therefore stopped teaching and for the next five years worked at Kibbutz Tel Adashim, in the Jezreel Valley. But even during her "pioneering" years Rachel Katznelson continued her literary and cultural activities. In 1919 she was called to Tel Aviv to become a member of the cultural committee of the newly founded Ahdut Avodah labor party and the following year was appointed to a similar position in Histadrut, the general federation of labor that had been formed by the Jewish workers in the country. She assumed the task of sending out adult education instructors to remote settlements and supplying kindergarten teachers to kibbutzim.

In 1920 she married Zalman Rubashow, who had been a classmate of hers at the Academy for Jewish Learning in St. Petersburg, and who was later to become better known as Zalman Shazar, the third President of the State of Israel.

Rachel Katznelson Rubashow became increasingly involved with the cultural activities of the women workers' movement. It was during this period that she edited the anthology *Divrei Poalot* (published in 1930) which was dedicated to the struggles and achievements of the Jewish woman worker in Palestine and of which *The Plough Woman* (published in 1932) is the English edition. The book was also translated into Yiddish, German and Bulgarian.

Impressed by the quality of the essays submitted by the women whom she had chosen to write for this anthology, she felt the need for a publication through which a working woman—seamstress, teacher, factory worker, kibbutznik or housewife—could develop her literary talents and express her views on the role of the wife and mother in the upbuilding of the Jewish Homeland. To this end in 1934 she founded a monthly journal, *D'var Hapoelet*, of which she was editor for the next 25 years and which became the main journal of the working women's movement in Israel.

During the 1930's she made several trips abroad, visiting the Pioneer Women's Organization in the United States and Canada and conducting a workers' seminar for the world HeHalutz movement in Poland only a year before that country was overrun by the Nazis.

Following World War II, she went to the D.P. camps of Germany to work with survivors of the Nazi holocaust who were eager to rebuild their lives in Eretz Yisrael. When the United Nations Special Committee on Palestine (UNSCOP) came to Jerusalem to decide the future of the Jewish Homeland Rachel Katznelson Shazar testified before that body on behalf of the women's organizations of the country.

In 1958, on Israel's tenth Independence Day, she was awarded the Israel Prize in the field of the social sciences for a "half century's work in the educational and cultural absorption of the working women in Israel."

In 1963 her husband, Zalman Shazar, succeeded the late Itzhak Ben Zvi as President of the State of Israel. During the years he served in that office, Rachel Katznelson Shazar was hostess at the President's Mansion and accompanied her husband on several trips abroad.

She is the author of numerous books. *T'nuat Hapoelet, Mifale-ha u-Sh'ifoteha* (The Projects and Aspirations of the Working Women's Movement) appeared in 1941. *Massot UR'shimot* (Essays and Notes), a volume of essays and literary criticism, won her the Joseph H. Brenner Prize in 1946. In 1964 she edited *Im Pa'ame HaDor* (In the Footsteps of a Generation), a two-volume anthology covering the first 25 years of *D'var Hapoelet*. Two years later came *Al Admat Ha'Ivrit* (On Hebrew Soil) and in 1969, *She-Livuni Ve-Einan* (My Companions Who Have Gone), a book of essays on women active in Israel's public life.

THE CONTRIBUTORS

The original editon of *The Plough Woman* contained no biographical information about the women whose writings are included in this volume. Many of the authors were not identified since they signed their articles only with their first names, or initials, in keeping with the spirit of the working women's movement, whose members were reluctant to claim personal credit for work in behalf of the common cause.

However, in the course of the four decades that have passed since the publication of the original edition of *The Plough Woman,* some of the writers have become prominent figures whose identities are of general interest. But because so many of these women and their contemporaries are no longer alive, our information is of necessity incomplete.

The following list includes only those who could be identified at this date.

DEVORAH BARON, a well-known writer and translator, was born in Belorussia in 1887. She published her first short story at the age of 15 in the Hebrew periodical *Hamelitz.* At the age of 23 she settled in Palestine, where she married the Labor Zionist leader and writer Joseph Aharonowitz (1877–1937). Her first anthology of short stories, *Sippurim,* was published in 1927. Most of her writings depict Jewish life in the small towns of Russia. In addition to her original work she translated Flaubert's *Madame Bovary* into Hebrew. In 1934 she was the first recipient of the Bialik Prize for literature. She died in Tel Aviv in 1957.

LILIA BASEVITCH, writer and educator, was born in Russia and settled in Palestine in her early youth. She became one of the leading members of Kibbutz Ein Harod and a member of the edi-

torial board of *D'var Hapoelet*, the monthly magazine published
by Moetzet Hapoalot (The Council of Women Workers) in Israel.

ESTHER (STURMAN) BECKER (later Esther Rainin), was born
in Yekaterinoslav, Russia, in 1891, and settled in Palestine in
1906. She was one of the founders of Kibbutz Merchavya, and
also helped found the Hashomer self-defense organization. She
was a member of the Sturman (Shturman) family, which has become legendary in the history of Jewish pioneering and in the
struggle for Jewish statehood. Her brother, Hayim Šturman,
who settled in Palestine with the rest of the family in 1906 and
was one of the founders of Kibbutz Ein Harod, was killed in
1938 by a land mine near an Arab village. His son, Moshe, was
killed in Israel's War of Independence, and Moshe's son Hayim
fell in 1969 in the Suez Canal area. Esther died in 1973.

SHIFRA (STURMAN) BETZER, elder sister of Esther Becker,
was born in 1885 and settled in Palestine in 1906. Together with
her husband Israel Betzer (1883–1963) she helped found Kibbutz Deganiah. She died in 1962.

REBECCA BROISMAN served for many years as principal of
the agricultural school run by the Moetzet Hapoalot in Petach
Tikvah.

CHAYA SARAH CHANKIN was born in Russia in 1882. Settling in Palestine in 1903, she was an early member of the Hashomer self-defense organization.

CHASIAH's full name is HASSIAH KUPERMINTZ-DRORI. A
member of Moshav K'far Yehezkel and veteran leader of the
working women's movement, she was at one time a member of
the Knesset, Israel's Parliament.

HANNAH CHISICK (CHIZHIK), initiator of the working women's communes, was born in Russia in 1891. She arrived in
Palestine in 1905 with her brother, Baruch, the first of a family

of ten, including her parents, to settle in the Jewish Homeland. In 1922 she founded a *meshek poalot* (training farm for pioneer women, see Glossary) in Nachlat Yehuda. During a period of widespread unemployment in 1926 she originated the idea of the chavurah or women workers' commune. From 1930 to 1931 she was in the United States as a delegate of Moetzet Hapoalot (The Council of Women Workers) in Israel to the Pioneer Women's Organization. She died in 1951.

ARAH CHISICK (CHIZHIK), sister of Hannah Chizhik, born in Russia in 1899, was brought to Palestine by her parents in 1906. She first worked on her parents' farm near Lake Kinneret and subsequently at various settlements. She was killed together with Joseph Trumpeldor at Tel Hai in 1920.

REBECCA DANITH was born in Russia in 1896. Settling in Palestine in 1913, she was one of the first women to work at highway construction near Tiberias and eventually became a member of Kibbutz Ein Harod. She died in 1954.

D.D.'s full name is DEBORAH DAYAN. Born in the Ukraine in 1891, she studied at the University of Kiev. Settling in Palestine in 1913, she joined Kibbutz Deganiah. In 1914 she married Shmuel Dayan. (Her elder son, Moshe, became Israel's Minister of Defense.) In 1921 Deborah Dayan and her husband were among the founders of the *moshav ovdim* Nahalal. She became known as a talented writer of short stories and was an editor of the women workers' magazine *D'var Hapoelet*. Her articles were collected in two anthologies; one of these was published in an English translation (*Pioneer*, 1968). She died in 1956.

JUDITH EDELMAN, born in the Ukraine in 1893, arrived in Palestine at the age of 20. She was one of the founders of G'dud HaAvodah ("Labor Battalion"), the elite pioneering group which sought to weld all the Jewish workers in Palestine into one great commune based on the common ownership of property and equality as consumers. She was also one of the founding members of Kibbutz Ein Harod. She died in 1959.

JAEL (YAEL) GORDON was born in Russia in 1879, the daughter of Aharon David Gordon, philosopher, pioneer and exponent of the "religion of labor" (see Glossary). She settled in Palestine in 1908, taught at various settlements and also engaged in agricultural work. She died in 1958.

RACHEL JANAITH (RACHEL YANAIT), wife of Itzhak Ben Zvi, Israel's second President, and a noted educator in her own right, was born in the Ukraine in 1886. A founder of the Labor Zionist movement during her student days in Kiev, she settled in Palestine in 1908. She helped found the Hebrew High School in Jerusalem and was one of the founders of the Hashomer self-defense organization. In 1918 she married Ben Zvi (1884–1963). In 1920 she established a plant nursery for women workers near Talpiyot, which later became an agricultural training school for girls. Also during the 1920's, she was responsible for the founding of the Pioneer Women's Organization in the United States. Pioneer women came into being when a group of women in the United States, in response to Rachel Yanait's request for aid, sent $500 to help pay for the digging of a well at the plant nursery. In 1927 she was in the United States as the delegate of Moetzet Hapoalot to Pioneer Women. In 1948 she established a youth village in Ein HaKerem. She is the author of numerous articles. Her autobiography, *Anu Olim* (1959), which describes her life from 1908 to 1917, was published in an English translation, *Coming Home* (1964).

R.K. is RACHEL KATZNELSON SHAZAR, the editor of this volume.

TECHIAH LIBERSON was born in Russia in 1888 and arrived in Palestine in 1905. One of the founders of Kibbutz Deganiah, she eventually settled in Nahalal.

G.M. is GOLDA MEIR, then Golda Myerson.

SARAH MALKIN was born in Russia in 1885 and settled in Palestine at the age of 20. One of the founders of Kibbutz Deganiah, she was engaged in child care work for some time and later was a nurse at the first hospital in Zikhron Yaakov for workers suffering from malaria. She died in 1949.

RACHEL (RACHEL BLOWSTEIN or BLUVSTEIN), the poet of the Second Aliyah, was born in Russia in 1890. Arriving in Palestine with her sister in 1909, she did agricultural work in Rehovot and at the girls' training farm in what is now Kibbutz Kinneret. It was in memory of those early pioneering days that she later composed her famous song *Ve-Ulai* ("Perhaps"). In 1913 she went to Toulouse, France, to study agriculture. At the outbreak of World War I she was ordered out of France and had to return to her native Russia. In 1919 she was able to go back to Palestine, but poor health prevented her from resuming the farm work she loved and she taught school in Jerusalem. She died in Tel Aviv in 1931 and was buried at Kibbutz Kinneret. Her early writings were in Russian but after 1920 she began to write poetry in Hebrew. An anthology of her poems, *Shirat Rahel*, was published posthumously in 1939.

REBECCAH is REBECCA BROISMAN (see above).

SHOSHANA RECHTHANT-JAFFE (JOFFE) was born in Poland in 1889. After arriving in Palestine in 1911 she worked in Petach Tikvah and Mikveh Israel. In the 1920's she settled in Nahalal, where she devoted her time to farming chores. She was married to the author and pioneer Eliezer Lipa Joffe (1882–1942), who served in the Jewish Legion during World War I and who helped found T'nuva, Israel's marketing cooperative for farm products, Shoshana Joffe died in 1956.

ZIPPORAH SEID (ZEID) was born in Vilna in 1892 and settled in Palestine in 1907. She married Alezander Zeid (1886–1938), one of the founders of the Hashomer self-defense organization. Despite her husband's death at the hand of Arab marauders, she continued in her efforts to promote good will between Jews and Arabs in Palestine.

MANYA WILBUSCHEWITZ-SHOCHAT, leader in Jewish self-defense and social worker, was born to a wealthy family in Russia in 1880. She joined the Russian social revolutionary movement but under the impact of the pogroms of the early 1900's she moved to Palestine in 1904 to join her brother Nahum Wilbuschewitz (see Glossary), who had gone there the preceding year. She and her husband, the lawyer Israel Shochat (1886–1961), were among the founders of the Hashomer self-defense organization. They later joined in the formation of Kibbutz K'far Gileadi. During World War I they were deported to Anatolia by the Turks. After their return to Palestine following the war, they settled in K'far Gileadi. During the 1920's and 1930's, Manya Shochat was active in Haganah, the self-defense force of Palestine's Jewish community and direct precursor of the Israel Defense Force of today. She visited the United States several times on behalf of the Labor Zionist movement. During World War II she helped bring "illegal" immigrants from Nazi-held Europe into Palestine. She spent the last years of her life assisting newcomers to Israel. She died in 1961.

EVA TABENKIN, born in Warsaw in 1889, joined the Labor Zionist movement during her high school days. In 1912, after having studied at the schools of philosophy and medicine of the University of Cracow, she settled in Palestine with her husband, the Labor Zionist leader Itzhak Tabenkin (1887–1971). She was one of the founding members of Kibbutz Ein Harod, where she took a special interest in educational work. She died in 1947.

TECHIAH is TECHIAH LIBERSON (see above).

NECHAMAH ZITZER (SITZER; also SAR-TZIYON) worker and writer, was born in Russia in 1891. In 1913 she settled in Palestine. She worked at various settlements. She was among the founders of a number of important Labor Zionist newspapers and was active in the working women's movement.

PERSONALITIES

ACHAD HA-AM (AHAD HA'AM; 1856–1927). Hebrew essayist and author of the idea of Palestine as a spiritual center of Judaism. He settled in Palestine in 1922.

ASH (ASCH, SHOLEM; 1880–1957), the Yiddish novelist and playwright.

AZEFF, YEVNO FISHELEVICH (1869–1918). Double agent who served the Czarist secret police and at the same time played a leading role in the Russian social revolutionary movement.

BARATZ, JOSEPH (1890–1968). Israeli pioneer and labor leader. Born in Russia, he settled in Palestine in 1906 and was one of the founders of Kibbutz Deganiah. His history of Deganiah has been published in an English translation, A *Village By the Jordan* (1954).

BARSKI, MOSES (1894?–1913). Early pioneer, killed by Arab marauders near Deganiah. Following his death, his entire family left their native Russia to settle in the Jewish Homeland. Moshe Dayan was named for him.

BATH MIRIAM, YOHEVED (1901–   ) well-known Hebrew poet. Born in Belorussia, she settled in Palestine in the late 1920's.

BERDITCHEVSKI, MICAH JOSEPH (BIN-GORION; 1865–1921), well-known Hebrew novelist.

BIALIK, HAYIM NACHMAN (1873–1934), the famous Hebrew poet.

BOGEN, SHOSHANA (1898–1918). Young woman pioneer. Born in Russia, she emigrated to Palestine at the age of 15.

BRENNER, JOSEPH CHAIM (1881–1921). Hebrew writer and pioneer in Palestine. Born in the Ukraine, he settled in Palestine in 1909, first working as a laborer, but later turning to journalism and becoming a leader in the Jewish workers' movement. His stories give a realistic picture of life in Palestine in his day. He was killed in the Arab riots of 1921. Kibbutz Givat Brenner is named after nim. His novel *Sh'kol V'Khishalon* (1920) was translated into English under the title *Breakdown and Bereavement* (1971).

BUSEL (BUSSEL), JOSEPH (1891–1919). One of the founders of Kibbutz Deganiah. Born in Russia, he came to Palestine in 1908.

CHABAS (HABAS), BERACHAH (1909–1968). Hebrew journalist and editor Born in Lithuania, she was brought to Palestine in 1907. One of her books, dealing with illegal immigration into Palestine, was published in an English translation *(The Gate Breakers*, 1963).

CHANKIN, EZEKIEL (1881–1913). Early pioneer in Palestine and one of the founders of the Hashomer self-defense organization. He was married to Chaya Sarah Chankin.

CHANKIN, (HANKIN), JOSHUA (1864–1945). Palestine pioneer and public servant. Born in the Ukraine, he was brought to Palestine by his parents, who were among the founders of Rishon LeZion. He was instrumental in the acquisition and settlement of large tracts of land, including the Emek Jezreel, and was popularly known as "The Redeemer of the Emek."

CHERNICHOVSKY (TSCHERNIKHOVSKI), SHAUL (1875–1943), the famous Hebrew poet and essayist. Born in Russia, he settled in Palestine in the 1930's.

DASHEVSKY, PiNCHAS (1879–1934). Russian Zionist activist. Born in an assimilated family, he joined a socialist Zionist students' group and later the Jewish self-defense organization in Kiev. He wounded Pavolachi Krushevan, the anti-Semitic newspaper editor who had instigated the Kishinev pogrom in 1903. After his release from prison, Dashevsky continued his work as a chemical engineer, remaining an active Zionist even after the Communist takeover in Russia. He was eventually arrested by the Soviet authorities and died in prison.

DIZENGOFF, MEIR (1861–1936). First mayor of Tel Aviv. Born in Russia, he settled in Palestine in 1892.

EINHORN, DAVID (1886–   ). Well-known Yiddish poet. Born in Russia, he lived variously in Switzerland, Germany, France and (after 1940) in the United States.

ELISHEVA (BIKHOWSKY, ELISHEVA; 1888–1949). Hebrew poet. Born a non-Jew in Russia, she came into contact with Jewish circles and was drawn into the movement for Jewish national rebirth. In 1920 she embraced Judaism and married the Hebrew writer Simon Bikhowsky, with whom she moved to Palestine five years later. In addition to poems and stories, her Hebrew writings include articles of literary criticism on Hebrew and European literature. She was popularly known as "Ruth from the banks of the Volga."

ENTOBY (ANTABI), ALBERT ABRAHAM (1869–1918). Educator. Born in Damascus, he was director of the educational institutions of the Alliance Israélite Universelle in Palestine.

FEIERBERG (FEUERBERG) MORDECAI Z'EV (1874–1899). Hebrew writer who lived in Russia. He began his literary career only some three years before his death from tuberculosis.

FISHMAN (MAIMON), ADA (1893–1973). Israeli pioneer, feminist leader and public servant. Born in Bessarabia, she settled in Palestine in 1912. She founded a girls' school in Safed, where she taught for some time. A leading figure in the struggle for women's rights, she was one of the earliest promoters of the Jewish working women's movement in Palestine and held prominent positions in the Histadrut and the world Zionist movement. From 1921 to 1930 she was secretary of the Moetzet Hapoalot, which she had helped organize. In 1930 she became principal of the women's agricultural high school in Ayanot. From 1949 to 1955 she represented Israel's Mapai party in the Knesset, the country's Parliament. She wrote several books on the Jewish working women's movement. One of them was published in English under the title *Women Build a Land* (1962).

GILEADI (GIL'ADI), ISRAEL (1886–1918). Early Palestine pioneer. Born in Bessarabia, he arrived in Palestine in 1905. He worked as a farmhand and in 1907 helped found the Hashomer self-defense organization. He planned and organized the founding of K'far Gileadi, which was subsequently named after him.

GISSIN ("Gissin's vineyard"). The Gissins were an early pioneering family in Palestine. Ephraim Gissin (1835–1898), an early member of Hoveve Zion, moved to Palestine from Belorussia in 1895 to join three sons and daughters who had settled in Petach Tikvah. One of his grandsons, Avshalom Gissin (1896–1921), was killed while defending Petach Tikvah against armed Bedouins.

GNESSIN, URI NISSAN (1881–1913). Hebrew novelist. Born in Russia, he lived there all his life except for a brief period in Palestine.

GORDON, AHARON DAVID (1856–1922). Ideological leader of the Jewish workers' movement in Palestine during the Second Aliyah. Born in Russia, he settled in Palestine at the age of 48, working as a farmhand in Petach Tikvah, Rishon LeZion and elsewhere in the country. He eventually settled in Kibbutz Deganiah, where he spent the rest of his life. He formulated what he called "the religion of labor," which idealized all physical work, especially the tilling of the soil, as an ultimate ethical value.

HIRSH, BARON (DE HIRSCH, BARON MAURICE; 1831–1896). Jewish philanthropist. In 1891 he founded the Jewish Colonization Association (ICA) to assist and promote the emigration of Jews from countries of oppression and to establish settlements for them in various parts of North and South America.

JABOTINSKY, VLADIMIR (1880–1940). Writer, orator, poet and founder of the Revisionist movement in Zionism.

KALUGAI, SHULAMITH (1891–1972). Hebrew writer and poet. Born in Russia, a sister of Itzhak Ben Zvi, later the second President of the State of Israel, she settled in Palestine about 1911.

KALVARISKI (KALWARISKI-MARGOLIS), CHAIM (1868–1947). Pioneer, agronomist and advocate of rapprochement between Jews and Arabs in Palestine. Born in Russian Poland, he settled in Palestine in 1895.

KRAUSE, ELIYAHU (1878–1962). Agronomist, born in Russia. In 1901 he became director of the training farm founded by the Jewish Colonization Association at Sedjera, where he was instrumental in the establishment of what was the first Jewish farm workers' cooperative in Palestine. For nearly 40 years, until his retirement in 1954, he was director of the Mikveh Israel agricultural school.

KRIGSER (AMIDAR), SARAH (STURMAN) (1888– ?). Early Palestine pioneer, sister of Esther Becker and Shifra Betzer, both of whom contributed articles to this volume.

KRUSHEVAN, PAVOLACHI (1860–1909). Russian anti-Semitic journalist who instigated the Kishinev pogrom with his inflammatory newspaper articles.

LISHANSKY, SARAH (1882–1924). Pioneer and health worker. Born in Russia, a sister of Rachel Yanait Ben Zvi, she joined the Socialist Zionist movement in Kiev. In 1909 she went with her family to Palestine. The last years of her working life were spent in Tel Aviv, where she administered the clinic maintained by Kupat Holim, the sick fund of Histadrut, the general federation of labor.

MAGNES, JUDAH L. (1877–1948). Rabbi and president of the Hebrew University. Born in the United States, he settled in Palestine in the 1920's. In 1942 he founded the Ihud organization, which advocated a binational Arab-Jewish state in Palestine, but he was unable to find Arab leaders willing to negotiate with the Jews.

MEISEL, HANNA (HANNA MEISEL-SHOCHAT) (1890–1972). Educator and world Zionist leader. Born in Russia, she settled in Palestine in 1909. There she founded training farms for girls (see Meshek Poalot) in Kinneret and subsequently in Nachlat Yehuda and Nahalal. She was principal of the Nahalal school from 1923 until 1960. In 1912 she married the labor leader Eliezer Schochat (1874–1971).

NISTOR (*DER NISTOR*, lit. "The Concealed One."). Pen name for Pinhas Kahanovitz (1884–1952), Russian Yiddish author. Arrested in the Stalinist purges, he died in a Russian prison hospital.

PERETZ, ISAAC LEIB (1851–1915). A major Hebrew and Yiddish author in Poland. Toward the end of his life he became the hero of the Yiddishist movement which championed Yiddish rather than Hebrew as the language of the Jewish people. His poems and stories depict small-town Hasidic life. One of his best-known stories is *Bontche Schweig*.

PINKERFELD, ANDA (known today as AMIR, ANDA; 1902–). Hebrew poet. Born in Galicia, she settled in Palestine in 1923. Following World War II she spent some time working with Holocaust survivors in displaced persons' camps in Germany. She is well known in Israel for her writings for juveniles.

PUCHATCHEVSKY, NECHAMAH (1869–1934). Writer and communal worker. Born in Russia, she joined the Hoveve Zion and settled in Palestine with her husband, a pioneer who worked for many years as an agricultural instructor. Her essays were published under the pen name of *Nefesh* ("Soul").

RAB (RAAB), ESTHER (1899–). Hebrew poet. Born in Palestine, the daughter of Judah Raab, one of the earliest settlers in Petach Tikvah, she eventually joined Kibbutz Deganiah.

RAISIN (REISEN), ABRAHAM (1876–1953). Yiddish poet. Born in Russia, he settled in the United States in 1886.

ROSENFELD, MORRIS (1862–1923). Yiddish poet. Born in Russia, he settled in the United States in 1886.

ROTHSCHILD, BARON EDMOND DE (1845–1934). French Jewish philanthropist. He saved the early modern Jewish settlements in Palestine from financial collapse. Though not a Zionist, he established the Palestine Jewish Colonization Association (PICA), which was to found more than 30 Jewish settlements in Palestine during his lifetime, and he developed various industries in the country.

RUTHBERG, MEYER (1887–1951). Palestine pioneer and founder of Hamashbir, the first economic agency established by the Jewish labor movement in Palestine. Born in the Ukraine, he settled in Palestine in 1905.

SALTZMAN, JOSEPH (d. 1913). Early Palestine pioneer. Born in Poland, he went to Palestine in 1907. There he helped found Kibbutz Kinneret. He was murdered by Arab marauders.

SHER, AARON (d. 1920). Palestine pioneer of the Second Aliyah. A member of Kibbutz Kinneret, he volunteered to help defend K'far Gileadi and Tel Hai and was one of the first to be killed in the Arab attack.

SHOCHAT, ELIEZER (1874–1971). Labor leader. Born in Russia, he was one of the earliest members of the Labor Zionist movement there. In 1904 he settled in Palestine with his brother, the lawyer Israel Shochat (husband of Manya Wilbuschewitz-Shochat). In 1912 he married Hanna Meisel. One of the first to develop the idea of the *moshav ovdim,* he helped found Nahalal.

SHOFMAN (SCHOFFMANN), GERSHON (1880– ?). Hebrew writer. Born in Belorussia, he fled to Galicia during the Russo-Japanese war. He edited a number of Hebrew literary journals in Poland and Austria before settling in Palestine in 1938.

SHOLOM ALEICHEM (1859–1916), the famous Jewish novelist and humorist. Born in the Ukraine, he emigrated to the United States. An early adherent of Zionism, he joined the Hoveve Zion in 1888. He helped found a Palestine settlement society in Kiev the following year and in 1890 helped organize the Odessa Committee for the support of Jewish agriculturists and artisans in Palestine. His Zionist writings include a biography of Theodor Herzl in Yiddish, two Yiddish pamphlets about Zionism, and a Zionist play, *David ben David,* which was published posthumously in 1959.

SZOLD, HENRIETTA (1860–1945). Educator, author, social worker, founder of Hadassah and organizer of Youth Aliyah.

TIOMKIN, VLADIMIR (1861–1927). Russian Zionist leader. In 1891 he became the first director of the Jaffa office of the Odessa Committee to support Jewish agriculturists and artisans in Palestine. He later returned to Russia. Subsequently, in Paris, he joined the Revisionist Zionist movement.

TRUMPELDOR, JOSEPH (1880–1920). Palestine pioneer and soldier. Born in Russia, he served in the Russian army during the Russo-Japanese war, in which he lost his left arm. While a prisoner of war in Japan he organized among his Jewish fellow prisoners a group of pioneers who intended to go to Palestine to engage in cooperative farming and to defend the Jewish settlements. He went to Palestine in 1912 and during World War I helped Vladimir Jabotinsky promote the idea of the Jewish Legion to help liberate Palestine from the Turks. He was killed in the Arab attack on TeJ Hai. The Revisionist Zionist youth organization B'rit Trumpeldor (Betar) is named after him.

WILBUSCHEVITZ, GEDALIAH (1865–1943). Mechanical engineer. Born in Russia (a brother of Manya Wilbuschewitz-Shochat), he settled in Palestine in 1892. He founded a metal casting and machine factory in Jaffa, the first Jewish enterprise of its kind in Palestine. His brother *Nahum* (1879–1971), also a mechanical engineer, settled in Palestine in 1903 and founded Atid, the first edible oil factory in Palestine which was located first in Ben Shemen and later in Haifa. Another brother, *Moshe* (1869–1952), a chemical engineer and inventor, settled in Palestine in 1919.

PLACES AND TERMS

ACHVAH (Lit. "Brotherhood"). Group of agricultural workers in Palestine in 1912. Employed in the orange orchards of Judea, they played a leading role in the movement for *Kibbush Avo-dah* ("Conquest of Labor"), which stressed the importance of Jewish labor as the basis for the new Jewish society that was to be built up in Palestine.

AFULA. Central city of the Jezreel Valley (see *Emek Jezreel*), founded in 1925 by the American Zion Commonwealth, an American Jewish organization formed for the purchase and development of land in Palestine for Jewish settlement.

AIN CHAROD (EIN HAROD). Kibbutz in the eastern Jezreel Valley, founded in 1921.

ALIYAH (Lit. "Ascent"). The immigration and settlement of Jews in Israel. Aliyah during the modern pioneering era prior to World War II (ca. 1882–1936) has been divided into five distinct periods; each had its own social and political influence on the development of what eventually became the State of Israel.

AYELETH HA-SHACHAR. Kibbutz in the Upper Galilee, founded in 1918 by Second Aliyah pioneers. Its population in 1970 was approximately 800.

BEERSHEBA. Principal city of the Negev. From a desert oasis Beersheba has grown into a flourishing city with a population of over 70,000. It is the home of Ben-Gurion University.

BETH ALPHA. Kibbutz in the Jezreel Valley, founded in 1922. Its population in 1970 was about 700.

CHALUKKAH (HALUKKAH; lit. "Distribution"). System of fund-raising outside Palestine for the support of needy pious Jews and full-time students of Talmudic law in Palestine. The Chalukkah way of life was rejected by the modern pioneers who came to Palestine to rebuild the Jewish Homeland by the work of their own hands.

CHALUTZ (HALUTZ; plural "Chalutzim" or "Halutzim"). A "pioneer" who settled in Palestine in order to help rebuild the Jewish Homeland by his own toil, particularly in agriculture.

CHAMARAH (HAMARAH). Tract of Jewish-owned land in the Upper Galilee. For a short time, it was an independent settlement but was later absorbed into K'far Gileadi.

CHATZBANI (HASBANI). Northernmost source of the Jordan River, in the Upper Galilee.

CHAVURAH (HAVURAH; lit. "Group;" plural, "Chavurot"). Women workers' commune active in Palestine during the middle and late 1920's.

CHEDERA (HEDERA). City in the northern Sharon Plain, about midway between Tel Aviv and Haifa, founded in 1890 in a swampy, dune-covered area by immigrants of the First Aliyah. Its population in 1970 was 30,000.

CHOVEVE ZION (HOVEVE ZION; "Lovers of Zion"). Pre-Zionist movement founded in 1882 for the purpose of encouraging Jews to settle in Palestine and to work for the revival of Jewish nationhood there.

COUNCIL OF WOMEN WORKERS or WORKING WOMEN'S COUNCIL (MOETZET HAPOALOT). Women's organization affiliated with the Histadrut, and concerned with issues of special interest to working women in Israel, such as the broadening of employment opportunities for women, the integration of women immigrants, vocational and agricultural training for women, family and child care, and the problems of working mothers. It maintains Mishke Poalot, working women's hostels, social and educational centers for single women immigrants, and children's homes, nurseries and kindergartens. It has long fought for the rights of women in every aspect of social, civic and political life. In 1930 it set up the Organization of Working Mothers, which established day care centers for pre-school youngsters. In 1934 the Moetzet Hapoalot founded *D'var Hapoelet,* the working women's monthly, whose long-time editor was Rachel Katznelson Shazar. (See also Epilogue to this volume by Beba Idelson).

DEGANIAH. Kibbutz in the Jordan Valley, founded in 1910. The first kibbutz in Israel, it is known as "the Mother of Kibbutzim." In 1970 the total population of Deganiah was about 1,000.

EFFENDI. Designation for high Turkish official or Arab landowner.

EMEK JEZREEL (Jezreel Valley). Valley linking the Mediterranean coast of Israel with the Jordan Valley. A malaria-ridden swamp for centuries, "the Emek," as it is popularly known, was purchased by the Jewish National Fund, and was settled and drained by Jewish pioneers in the 1920's. Eventually, the Jezreel Valley became the most fertile and densely settled region in the country.

FELLAH (Plural: "Fellaheen"). Arabic term denoting an individual who makes a living from farm work, regardless of whether he owns the land which gives him his livelihood.

FULEH. Arabic name for the site on which the city of Afula was built.

GER (lit. "Stranger"). Hebrew term denoting a Gentile convert to Judaism.

GIVATH SHLOSHAH (Actually, GIVAT HaSHLOSHAH). Kibbutz in central Israel, near the city of Petach Tikvah, founded in 1925. The population of the Kibbutz in 1970 was about 500.

HAHORESH. First Jewish workers' organization in the Galilee, founded at Sedjera for the purpose of training Jewish pioneers to do agricultural work.

HAMASHBIR. First economic agency established by the Jewish labor movement in Palestine. Founded in 1916 under the leadership of Meir Ruthberg during the economic crisis set off by World War I, it is today the main wholesale supplier for Israel's kibbutzim and consumers' cooperatives. Officially known today as HaMashbir HaMerkazit, it is affiliated with Histadrut.

HASHOMER (Lit. "Watchman"). First self-defense organization of the Jewish pioneers of the Second Aliyah, founded in Sedjera in 1909 to protect Jewish settlements from Arab marauders.

HASHOMER HATZAIR. Jewish youth movement first formed in 1913 in Galicia and Poland. The first pioneers from Hashomer Hatzair left for Palestine in 1919, and the organization eventually founded its own federation of kibbutzim. By the late 1920's the movement had become an international organization. Ideologically, it is affiliated with the left-wing socialist Mapam party.

HAURAN. Region in northeast Trans-Jordan, today part of Syria.

HAVER (Fem., "Havera"; Plural: "Haverim; Haverot.") "Comrade;" Term of address used for members of Kibbutzim and pioneer Zionist movements.

HEFZIBAH. Kibbutz in the eastern Jezreel Valley, near Beth Alpha, founded in 1922. The population of Hefzibah in 1970 was about 500.

HERZLIAH. City on the Mediterranean coast of Israel, north of Tel Aviv, founded in 1924 by the American Zion Commonwealth (see also Afula). The economy of the city is based on farming (particularly citriculture) and industry. It is also a popular health and vacation resort. During the first 20 years of Israel's existence, the population of Herzliah grew from 5,000 to 35,600.

HISTADRUTH (HISTADRUT). Israel's general federation of labor. It was formally established in Haifa in 1920. Histadrut is unique among labor federations in two respects: (1) It includes in its ranks not only hired workers but also self-employed individuals, housewives, and others who do not generally engage hired labor, and (2) while it is a federation of labor, it is also the largest single employer of labor in the State of Israel. Its activities include a health insurance plan, a youth organization, a network of vocational schools, the Ohel Theater and other cultural endeavors, a publishing house and a daily newspaper, *Davar*.

HULEH. Valley in the north of Israel. Originally a malarial swamp, it was first settled by Jews in the 1930's. Today the swamps and the lake originally in this area have been eliminated and the Huleh Valley has become one of the most fertile regions in Israel. The lower parts of the valley are utilized for fishponds and today contain almost half of all fishpond areas in the country.

ICA. See Jewish Colonization Association.

JABNIEL. One of the first Jewish settlements in the Galilee, founded by the Palestine Jewish Colonization Association (PICA) in 1901. An early center of the Hashomer Jewish self-defense organization, it was frequently attacked by Arab marauders in the beginning. The community engages in mixed farming, vegetable gardening, citriculture and viticulture. Its population in 1970 was over 1,500.

JAFFA. One of the oldest cities in Palestine. Its modern Jewish community developed in the late 19th century. Today Jaffa and Tel Aviv (which started out as a garden suburb of Jaffa) form the twin cities of Tel Aviv-Yafo.

JENIN. Arab town in Samaria in the West Bank area. It served as a base for Arab attacks on Jewish villages in the Jezreel Valley. In 1948 it was annexed by the Hashemite Kingdom of Jordan. Jenin was occupied by Israeli forces in the Six-Day War of 1967.

JEWISH COLONIZATION ASSOCIATION (ICA). Jewish philanthropic organization founded in 1891 by Baron Maurice De Hirsch with the aim of establishing East European Jews in agricultural settlements in Palestine. It supported various agricultural and educational institutions there.

JEWISH LEGION. Jewish military units formed by volunteers from Palestine, the United States, England, Canada and Argentina during World War I to fight alongside British troops for the liberation of Palestine from Turkish rule.

JEWISH NATIONAL FUND. Fund set up by the World Zionist Organization for the purchase, reclamation and afforestation of land in Palestine.

JEZREEL VALLEY. See Emek Jezreel.

KARKUR. Township in the central sector of the Mediterranean coastal plain of Israel.

K'FAR EZEKIEL (K'FAR YEHEZKEL). Moshav in the Emek Jezreel, founded in 1921.

K'FAR GILEADI. Kibbutz in the Upper Galilee, founded in 1916 by members of Hashomer to secure the northern frontier of Palestine against marauders. In 1920 K'far Gileadi and the neighboring settlement Tel Hai were attacked by Arabs. Its population in 1970 was about 700.

K'FAR TABOR. Village in the Lower Galilee, southwest of Tiberias, founded in 1901. Its population in 1970 was a little over 300.

KINERETH (KINNERET). Second oldest kibbutz in Israel, southeast of Lake Kinneret. It started out in 1908 as a training farm for Jewish laborers. In 1912 a girls' agricultural training farm was added, under the direction of Hanna Meisel-Shochat. That year, too, a group of pioneers arrived and eventually developed the settlement into a kibbutz. Among the pioneers who worked at the kibbutz prior to and during World War I were many who later achieved prominence in Israeli public life, including David Ben-Gurion and Shmuel Dayan. The economy of the kibbutz today is based on agriculture. Its population in 1970 was about 700.

KINERETH (KINNERET). Village on the southwest shore of Lake Kinneret, founded in 1909 by the Jewish Colonization Association. It has tourist hotels and restaurants; its economy is based on intensive farming. Its population in 1970 was close to 200.

KISHINEFF (KISHINEV) POGROM. Anti-Jewish outbreak in the Bessarabian city of Kishinev in April, 1903 in which almost 50 Jews were murdered, hundreds injured, and hundreds of Jewish homes and shops were looted. The pogrom triggered a sharp increase in Jewish emigration from Russia to America and Palestine, and stirred up Jewish nationalist sentiment among young Jews in much of Europe.

KVUTZAH. Today, this term is used interchangeably with "kibbutz." In the early pioneering days, however, it denoted a smaller, more selective and intimate group than the larger kibbutz.

LABOR DAILY. *Davar*, the daily newspaper published by the Histadrut from 1925 on. Among its early editors were Berl Katznelson (1887-1944) and Zalman Shazar (1889–1974), who was to become the third President of the State of Israel.

MASHBIR. See Hamashbir.

MERCHAVIAH (Merhavya). Village founded in 1911 in the

Emek Jezreel as a workers' agricultural settlement. In 1929 its place was taken by a kibbutz group affiliated with Hashomer Hatzair. A moshav by the same name was founded on land nearby in 1922 by a group of Jewish settlers from Russia. The population of the kibbutz in 1970 was about 560.

MESCHAH. See K'far Tabor.

MESHEK POALOT (lit. "Women Workers' Farm"). Name for training farms developed in Palestine for pioneer girls during the years immediately following World War I. The Mishke Poalot today are maintained by Moetzet Hapoalot.

METULAH (M'TULA). Village on the Lebanese border, founded in 1896. The population of Metulah in 1970 was about 400.

MIKVEH ISRAEL. Agricultural school near Tel Aviv. Founded in 1870 by the Alliance Israélite Universelle, a Jewish philanthropic, educational and civic defense organization with headquarters in Paris, Mikveh Israel was the first institution of its kind in Palestine and gave employment to early pioneers who arrived in the country in the 1880's. In the century that has passed since its inception, the school has trained thousands of Jewish agriculturists and made a vital contribution to the development of agriculture and agricultural research in Israel. It includes botanical gardens, a soil research station and an agricultural museum.

MILCHAMIAH (MENAHEMIYA). Moshav in the Jordan Valley. Founded in 1902, it was the first Jewish settlement in the Jordan Valley.

MOETZET HAPOALOT. See Council of Women Workers.

MOSHAV, MOSHAV OVDIM. Type of cooperative settlement in Israel. Like the kibbutz, it is based on the principle of self-labor, cooperation and mutual aid. Major agricultural machinery is owned by the moshav as a whole. The produce is marketed and supplies are bought cooperatively. The moshav differs from the kibbutz in that there is no communal kitchen or dining hall, and that each member is assigned a plot of land which he works by himself or with the help of members of his family living with him on the moshav. The ideal prototype of the moshav in its present form is Nahalal, which was established in 1921.

NABLUS (SH'CHEM). Biblical town in the West Bank area annexed by the Hashemite Kingdom of Jordan during the War of Independence. It was occupied by Israeli forces in the Six-Day War of 1967. There is a settlement of Samaritans at the western edge of the city.

NACHLATH JEHUDA (NACHLAT YEHUDA). Moshav in the central sector of Israel, founded in 1914 by the Hoveve Zion group of Odessa, Russia. In 1922 Hanna Meisel-Shochat founded a Meshek Poalot there. The population of the moshav in 1970 was about 2,400.

NAHALAL. Moshav in the western Jezreel Valley. It was founded in 1921 as the first settlement of the moshav or moshav ovdim type by a group from Kibbutz Deganiah. Among the founders of Nahalal were Shmuel and Deborah Dayan. A Meshek Poalot was founded there by Hanna Meisel-Shochat. In 1970 the population of the moshav, including the Meshek Poalot, was about 1,020.

NATIONAL FUND. See Jewish National Fund.

NESHER CEMENT FACTORY. Founded in Haifa soon after World War I

OHEL THEATRE. Workers' theater founded in Tel Aviv in 1925 under the auspices of the Histadrut.

PALESTINE JEWISH COLONIZATION ASSOCIATION (PICA). Established in 1924 by Baron Edmond de Rothschild as an entity separate from the Jewish Colonization Associatior (ICA) to support Jewish settlements, institutions and industria enterprises in Palestine.

PETACH TIKVAH. City on the Mediterranean coastal plain of Israel, northeast of Tel Aviv. Founded in 1878 as the first Jewish agricultural settlement in modern times, it became the first privately owned and operated farming village in modern Palestine. The Second Aliyah, however, brought many Jewish immigrant workers to Petach Tikvah and eventually the town became known as a center of the Jewish workers' movement. During the first two decades following the establishment of the State of Israel, the population of Petach Tikvah grew from about 22,000 to 75,000.

PURIAH (PORIYYA). Village in northern Israel near Tiberias. The original settlement on the site was founded in 1912 by a group of Zionists from the United States as a fruit farm, mainly based on almond planting. It was abandoned during World War I. The present village was founded on the site in 1949 by Yemenite immigrants.

RECHOBOTH (REHOVOT). Town in the Judean plain, south of Tel Aviv. Founded in 1890 by the Hoveve Zion of Warsaw and a group of other immigrants, Rehovot, which was self-supporting from the start, became a social and cultural center for the pioneers of the Second Aliyah. Rehovot today is a major industrial town and the seat of the Weizmann Institute of Science. Its population in 1970 was over 36,000.

ROSH PINAH. Village in the eastern Upper Galilee, founded on land bought in 1878 by a group of Jews from Safed. The population of Rosh Pinah in 1970 was about 825.

SAMARIA. Northern part of the central highlands of Palestine, annexed by the Hashemite Kingdom of Jordan during the War of Independence and occupied by Israeli forces during the Six-Day War.

SEDJERA (Present name: ILANYA). Village in the Lower Galilee, founded in 1902. This settlement was the birthplace of the Hahoresh workers' organization and the Hashomer self-defense organization. The site of the original Hashomer farm is now occupied by a school and youth center. The population of Ilanya in 1970 was about 180.

SEPHARDIC JEWS. Jews whose ancestors lived in Spain or Portugal before the expulsion of the Jews from those countries in 1492. Until 1882 most of Palestine's Jews were Sephardim. Eventually, however, they were outnumbered by Ashkenazic and Oriental Jews and by 1970 they comprised only about 5 per cent of Israel's total Jewish population.

SCHECHUNATH BORUCHOV (Actually: SH'HUNAT BORO-CHOV). Workers' suburb of Tel Aviv named for the theoretician of the Socialist Zionist movement, Ber Borochov (1881-1917). A Meshek Poalot was established there during the 1920's.

SHEIKH ABRIK (SHEIKH ABREK). Settlement in the Emek Jezreel, founded in 1925 by members of the Hapoel Hamizrachi (religious Labor Zionist) organization.

SHOMER. See Hashomer.

TEl ADAS (Actually: TEL ADASHIM). Moshav in the Emek Jezreel, north of Afula. It was established in 1923 by veterans of Hashomer and Jewish pioneers from Eastern Europe on the site of what had once been a Hashomer camp. The population of Tel Adashim in 1970 was about 400.

TEL AVIV. Largest city in Israel, founded in 1909 as an all-Jewish garden suburb of Jaffa. By 1921 the suburb had become an independent township and in 1934 was granted municipal status. Its population in 1970 was 384,000.

TEL HAI. Settlement in the Upper Galilee. Founded in 1918 as a camp for shepherds, it was in the area controlled by the French during the period immediately following World War I. In February, 1920, Arabs attacked the Jews of Tel Hai. Among the Jewish defenders killed in the attack were Sarah Chizhik and Joseph Trumpeldor.

300

TERRITORIALISTS. Members of Jewish movements to settle
Jews in a territory other than Palestine, with cultural, religious
and, if possible, political autonomy.

TIBERIAS. Town on the west shore of Lake Kinneret. During the
first two decades following the establishment of the State of Israel, the population of Tiberias grew from about 6,000 to 23,500.
It is the traditional resting place of many Jewish scholars, including Maimonides, and is a famous health and vacation resort;
its hot springs are frequented by visitors suffering from rheuma-
tism and related disorders.

TUL KEREM. Arab town east of Natanya. In 1920 a farm school
was established there with a bequest from the Jewish philanthropist Sir Elly Kadoorie. Annexed by the Hashemite Kingdom of
Jordan in 1949, Tul Kerem was occupied by Israeli forces during
the Six-Day War of 1967.

YEMENITES. The first substantial migrations of Jews from Yemen to Palestine occurred in 1881–2 and 1905. In 1910 the
Palestine Office of the World Zionist Organization sent to Yemen a Russian-born representative, Shmuel Yavneli, to organize
large-scale Jewish migration to Palestine. Between 1949 and
1950 almost the entire Jewish community of Yemen was transferred to Israel in "Operation Magic Carpet."

ZICHRON JACOB (ZIKHRON YA'AKOV). Village on the
southern slopes of Mt. Carmel, founded in 1882 by settlers from
Rumania and initially aided by Baron Edmond de Rothschild. It
has become a popular tourist resort. Its population in 1970 was
about 5,000.

PIONEER WOMEN, the Women's Labor Zionist Organization of America, was founded in New York in 1925 to promote the national and social ideals of Labor Zionism in Israel and in the United States.

Pioneer Women has chapters in most of the major cities in the United States, committed to the same ideals around which the organization was founded: the equality of women, the dignity of labor, the importance of the Jewish Homeland and the continuity of Jewish life in the United States. Pioneer Women is the sister organization of Moetzet Hapoalot, the Working Women's Council in Israel. Its basic program is:

(1) To train and educate Israeli women to lead full productive lives, and to provide the social services and educational tools needed to achieve this goal.

(2) To educate American Jewish women for a more active involvement in Jewish communal life and in the establishment of a more egalitarian and progressive society in the United States.

In Israel, Pioneer Women operates a large network of social service installations for the women, children and young people of the country.

In the United States, Pioneer Women actively supports Jewish educational activities, youth programs and community agencies.

Pioneer Women also maintains close contacts with sister groups in Canada, Argentina, Australia, Brazil, Chile, France, Belgium, Great Britain, Mexico, Peru and Uruguay, which are similarly dedicated to Jewish education and culture, the promotion of social legislation, and the protection of Jewish rights in general and women's rights in particular.

National Headquarters:

315 Fifth Avenue

New York, N.Y. 10016